# TINY
# HOT DOGS

All of these stories are true-ish, except for the parts that are not.

Running Press
Hachette Book Group
1290 Avenue of the Americas, New York, NY 10104
www.runningpress.com
@Running_Press

Printed in the United States of America

First Edition: April 2019

Published by Running Press, an imprint of Perseus Books, LLC, a subsidiary of Hachette Book Group, Inc. The Running Press name and logo is a trademark of the Hachette Book Group.

The Hachette Speakers Bureau provides a wide range of authors for speaking events. To find out more, go to www.hachettespeakersbureau.com or call (866) 376-6591.

The publisher is not responsible for websites (or their content) that are not owned by the publisher.

Print book cover design by Rodrigo Corral.
Interior design and illustration by Joshua McDonnell.

Library of Congress Control Number: 2018961684

ISBNs: 978-0-7624-6556-9 (hardcover), 978-0-7624-6555-2 (ebook)

LSC-C

10   9   8   7   6   5   4   3   2   1

# TINY
# HOT DOGS

## a memoir
## in small bites

# MARY
# GIULIANI

RUNNING PRESS
PHILADELPHIA

IN JOYFUL MEMORY OF
MY GRANDMOTHERS,
MARY AND LUCILLE

# CONTENTS

Pizza in a Cup

My Bat Mitzvah

Playing "Johnny Carson"

Hong Kong Flu

Put Your Socks and Your Panties On

What's a Patagonia?

Italian Hot Dogs

# Part II: Cigarettes

## Things Are Going To Start Happening To Me Now. . . . 45

# Part III: Cocktails

# INTRODUCTION:
# TINY HOT DOGS

The term *pigs in a blanket* often refers to hot dogs or Vienna, cocktail, or breakfast/link sausages wrapped in biscuit, pancake, or croissant dough and then baked. The first written record of pigs in a blanket occurs in *Betty Crocker's Cookbook for Boys and Girls* in 1957. For a small kid, they can be a full meal. Most adults do not admit to enjoying them as much as they do.

When I was eight years old, my father came home with a VCR—which, if you don't remember, was the size of a Cadillac—and a VHS tape of Carl Reiner's film *The Jerk*.

I'm crossing my fingers that most of you have seen *The Jerk*. If not, I beg you to drop this book (please not in the store but preferably at home after you've made your purchase) and watch this cinematic masterpiece. Or here's a quick synopsis: In *The Jerk*, Navin Johnson (played by Steve Martin) is a hugely delusional optimist who believes he was born a poor black child in Mississippi. He was not; he is actually white. Upon hearing a song on the radio, he is inspired to leave his loving and overprotective family and head out on an adventure to "be somebody." Shortly into his journey, he lands a job at a gas station in St. Louis and is thrilled to discover his name printed in the new phone book. This is a watershed moment for him—a defining point in his existence, if you will—and gives him the courage to embark on one misadventure to another as he dodges gunfire, joins the carnival, invents gadgets, becomes a millionaire, and finds love in the arms of his beautiful girlfriend, Marie, played by the great Bernadette Peters.

Why is this important? Because Navin Johnson is my hero. While my other friends at the time were listening to Wham! and waking up before they go-go'd, I was watching *The Jerk*—every night. This went on for an entire year. I became the sole student in the Academy of Navin Johnson. I chose at a very early age to be, like Navin, *optimistically delusional*.

Navin was also the first person to properly encapsulate exactly how I felt growing up in that I deeply loved my family and the town in which I grew up but felt an enormous disconnect from both. Like Navin, who was white and wanted to be black, I was Italian and wanted to be Jewish. I grew up in Great Neck, Long Island, a suburb located about eighteen miles from New York City. Population breakdown when I was growing up: 99 percent Jewish. Exceptions to that demographic: my Jesus-loving, al-dente-spaghetti-eating Italian family.

Pause. I think I need to explain the kind of Italians my family—which included my mom, my dad, my perfectly styled for the 1980s older sister, and an assortment of grandparents—was. We were not the second-generation kind that speaks Italian beautifully, cans their own sauce in the garage, or visits cousins in Tuscany every summer. No, we're third-generation Italian. We quote *Goodfellas* like scripture, we call tomato sauce "the sauce," we speak *Godfather I* and *II* Italian, we enjoy white leather in the summer, and we are most comfortable when the bride and groom enter their wedding reception via a fog pit with the theme from *Rocky* playing.

To add insult to injury, puberty was not my friend. In those formative years, the nickname bestowed upon me by my "friends" was Macchio Kahlo. Macchio, because I resembled Ralph Macchio in his breakaway role in the smash film *Karate Kid*, which was the number-one movie around the world for eighteen months. And Kahlo, because I had one eyebrow, and, lucky for me, there was a kid in my class who took an early interest in art history.

Note: I know some of you (my mother) are thinking that I was unique and special in a darling way. That I was kooky and lovable. Wrong. This was pre–Lena Dunham. Unique and special weren't celebrated back then. This was 1985, and I was just the weird girl who sang "The Thermos Song" from *The Jerk* aloud to no audience.

Second note: when I say "no audience," I mean that literally. I had very few friends, unless of course you count my hero, my Papa Charlie, a.k.a. my best friend, who loved four things equally: cocktails, cigarettes, Carvel ice cream, and me. His wife, my Grandma Mary (my namesake), had Alzheimer's disease, so while Papa and I were dressing up as a cadre of aging 1970s TV stars (we loved watching *The Love Boat* and *Fantasy Island* in costume), Grandma could often be found vacuuming our front lawn in her nightgown or attempting to cook the Thanksgiving turkey in our linen closet.

So here I am: friendless, hairy, *deeply* uncool. And not Jewish—*so* not Jewish. And I really tried. I wanted to be Jewish so badly that I electively went to Hebrew school with my best friend, Lauren. I attended so often that I can recite the entire hoftorah, and I'm fairly certain I was the only Italian eight-year-old who looked into the Shabbos Goy program at the nearby Long Island Jewish Hospital. When my father asked me what that was and I replied, "You know. Shabbos Goy . . . I'm going to push the elevator buttons for the Orthodox Jews at the hospital on Saturdays,"

I was met with a double helping of that look parents reserve for their most worrisome child, the one about whom they're just not sure.

On the rare days the kids called me by my real name, Mary, I almost longed for the moniker Macchio Kahlo because the name Mary was yet one more reminder of just how far from Jewish I was. (Sidebar: I would gladly accept being called Macchio these days instead of the man I am mistaken for on a daily basis: former Mayor of New York City, Rudy Giuliani! For the record, It's Mary not Mayor!

Back to my one eyebrow. I was so uncool that other people's parents took pity on me and forced their kids to invite me to all the parties. So in 1986, I attended 178 bar/bat mitzvahs. Picture, if you will, a unibrowed Ralph Macchio dressed in a poufy pink dress attending two or three of these soirees a weekend.

Where was Macchio Kahlo during these extravagant rites of passage? Not being pursued by a cute boy name Seth from Syosett. Not holding hands with Ali Cohen and all the cool girls during the Horah circle. Nope. Macchio Kahlo could be found, Sabbath after Sabbath, parked outside the door to the caterer's kitchen, waiting for the silver tray of those shiny, buttery, salty, perfect little tiny hot dogs also known as pigs in a blanket. I guess you could say, this is where the love affair began.

Fast-forward to 1997. Macchio Kahlo graduated Georgetown University (another place I didn't really belong) and arrived in New York to pursue another highly unattainable dream: an acting career. Yes, I was going to be an actress. I was going to make it in the city that never sleeps. How did it go? Put it this way . . . I had a better chance of being Jewish. The closest I ever got to stardom was hanging Lorne Michael's coat while working at celebrity mecca Nobu during a short stint as a coat check attendant. But I approached every small gig or audition as my next big break, blindly and happily guided by my wildly unrealistic optimism until it ran dry.

Defeated and broke, I answered an ad in the *New York Times* for a sales position at a catering company that boasted clients in the arts, fashion, and entertainment. Little did I know that this job, which I took with no greater aspiration than to no longer bounce checks at Blockbuster Video, would end up being my greatest role.

Here I was reunited with that silver tray containing my salty, buttery, glistening little friends . . . those tiny hot dogs. Very quickly I decided to trade in one dream for another and follow that tray, maybe not literally, like I did when I was thirteen around bedazzled event spaces, but in a real way. Real for me, at least. I stopped worrying about when I'd get my big break on Broadway. I stopped worrying about being/looking/acting like everyone else. I stopped worrying about what I had to do with my big fancy degree.

And oh, the places we would go, me and those tiny hot dogs on a silver tray. This tray took me to parties where I would meet Sophia Loren, Jay-Z, and Beyoncé, onto billionaires' yachts, into Kevin Klein's living room (while he was preparing for the role of Cole Porter), and even into Carolina Herrera's kitchen behind her kitchen. (Yes, that's a real thing.)

Ultimately, my "Navintude," as I've come to call it, and those tiny hot dogs gave me the chutzpah to create my business, cook grilled cheese with the Barefoot Contessa, dine on a Caesar salad with Robert De Niro, and cause Jimmy Fallon to laugh so hard that he spit out his wine. It also helped me become a mom (after eleven doctors told me I couldn't) and laugh in the face of that William Morris agent who said I didn't have "a face for TV" every time I'm on *The Rachael Ray Show*.

Listen, it has not been as easy as it sounds. Like Navin, I stumbled over obstacles—both in my personal and professional life—that even my sunny optimism couldn't clear. But also like Navin, I saw adventures even in my misadventures and came out on top—or at least I came out laughing.

To all of this, I smile and keep on moving, but, just between you and me, occasionally I do sit and ponder, Am I talented, am I lucky, or am I just *The Jerk?*

**PART I:**

# CARVEL

## THE WONDER YEARS

# Pizza in a Cup

I first watched Carl Reiner's film, *The Jerk*, starring Steve Martin, when I was eight years old, and it changed nearly everything about my sweet suburban life (let's go with "for the better," although I suppose you should read this and decide for yourself).

As I was watching *The Jerk* nearly nightly and well past my bedtime, mornings were rough. They would usually begin with my mother shaking me violently, pulling off the covers, and yelling at me to brush my hair and teeth, get dressed, and come to breakfast.

Eventually I would make it to the breakfast table, where my sister, Nanette—whose perfect barrettes matched her perfect dress (perfectly)—would be finishing the last few bites of her cereal while quietly reading another American classic (electively). Nanette my mother understood, whereas she often looked at me with love, yes, mixed with something

2

mystified, like "Really? *This* came out of *me*?" as she shook her head and prodded me to finish my pancakes. A honk in the driveway, and there was Bus 24 idling by our house, waiting to take us on our long journey, forty-five minutes away, to the next town and to school.

We lived in Great Neck, Long Island, a predominately Jewish neighborhood, and we couldn't be more Italian if we tried. My father had a moustache (as did my sister and I). Since neither yeshiva nor the public school down the street was an option, my parents sent my sister and me to the Catholic school in a neighboring town, where we were the only students from Great Neck and were thus quickly labeled "those weird girls."

I dreaded every minute of that forty-five-minute bus ride. My sister would always get on the bus before me, take the first seat to the right, and bury her face back in her book. I would follow behind, with my crazy hair, half dressed in a dirty uniform with pancake syrup on the side of my face. But unlike Nanette, I opted for the back of the bus. Since we were the only students on the entire bus who came from another town, we were mysterious, and with mystery came a lot of whispers, stares, and speculation. We were teased and made fun of relentlessly, until one day I realized that since there was already a big mystery surrounding who we were, it was my obligation to fill in the gaps. If we were going to be the talk of the bus, I was going to give them something to talk about.

My exaggerations (okay, lies) were easy to get away

with, as my sister had mastered the art of ignoring me and mostly stuck to her studies. So while I held court in the back of the bus "big fishing" it, my sister was conveniently too far away to interfere. The film *The Jerk* served as the inspiration for my tall tales.

Me: "Yes, Anna Maria Russo, we have a bathtub shaped like a clam and a red billiards room."

"What's a billiards room?" a boy named Tom would ask.

"It's a place to play pool and where you display your stuffed camel collection."

As "wows" and "ahs" and "what elses" were thrown my way, I was *loving* the attention.

"Mary, do you really have a tennis court and a pool?"

"I have *three* pools, Vinny, and a water cooler that dispenses red and white wine, and sometimes I sneak a little vino."

This went on for weeks, the crowd on the bus growing larger each day. At one point, I had the entire bus believing that I had a disco in my basement, that my father drove a yellow Lamborghini, and that I had a dog named Shithead who could smell danger from miles away.

And then one day, the unthinkable happened: a girl at school actually wanted to have a playdate with me! Me, the girl with one eyebrow from a faraway town who smelled like pancake syrup. I remember being excited and terrified at the same time. I quickly told her yes, and a date was set.

In the days leading up to her arrival, I did my best to fill in the gaps between my boasting and reality. I put two blow-up pools next to our existing in-ground pool (I never told them what kind). I begged my cousin Scott to bring over his mini pool table and created a makeshift billiards room in my basement. I put a blinking flashlight in our spare "junk" room, stuck a tape in my boom box, and poof! I had a disco.

My mother asked what I was doing as I moved a fern from the living room into my bedroom to create a jungle for my "pet monkey." I told her I was setting up for my friend Anne Marie's arrival.

"Mom, please please please please serve us our pizza in a cup like in *The Jerk*!" I pleaded. The Look, a muttered response, and she returned to the kitchen.

When Anne Marie arrived for our playdate, I was panicked. I took her quickly on a tour of the house to see all the things I had fabricated, making excuses for why Iron Balls McGinty (my bodyguard and another character from my beloved film) wasn't there to play with us and how the arcade I'd boasted about having, with its very own Ms. Pac-Man machine, had been destroyed in "the flood."

"It was just terrible, Anne Marie, just terrible. Our giraffe drowned in that flood, too."

Slowly Anne Marie started to realize that the only thing drowning was me in my sea of lies. In the nick of time, my mother called us upstairs for lunch. She had cut up our pizza and put the pieces into little cups with forks, just as I had described. Anne Marie smiled, sat down, and began to eat her lunch.

I sat there waiting for her to get mad or angry, to call me a liar, to tell me that she was going to expose me to the entire school. I waited and waited as, piece by piece, Anne Marie quietly noshed each bite of her pizza in a cup.

When she was done she placed the empty cup down, looked at me, and said, "Mary, this pizza is really good. Can I come back tomorrow?"

My lucky break with Anne Marie created a monster; because from then on I was deeply wedded to the idea that my fantasy life would always trounce the real world. I've continued to believe this theory to this day, which explains why I've made a pretty nice living creating unique party experiences for clients who have seen it all. I encourage those on the fence, whose imagination is perhaps . . . lacking . . . that turning their garage into a disco is always a great idea, or I encourage them to take a chance by serving only hot dogs and martinis at their next soiree, and when I suggest that we try to contact the real Elton John to play at the end of their event for the ultimate party *Wow!*, I really do believe I can make that happen. Point is, nothing is impossible. If you can dream it, you can do it (or at least some variation of it, like my makeshift billiards room).

Many years later, at the moment I felt I had finally "made it," I went on eBay and purchased my very own Ms. Pac-Man machine. Anne Marie, feel free to stop on by anytime and take me up on that game I promised you thirty-five years ago.

# Deconstructed Pizza Skewers with Roasted Tomato, Fried Mozzarella, and Basil Aioli

As good as I am, it's quite hard to convince my clients to eat pizza out of a cup, so here is how I pay homage to my favorite childhood meal.

### MAKES 24 PIECES

¾ cup light mayonnaise

⅓ cup basil leaves

¼ cup baby arugula leaves

1 tablespoon fresh lemon juice

1½ teaspoon minced garlic

1 tablespoon grated Parmesan

Salt and pepper to taste

1 half-pint container red or yellow grape tomatoes

1 package small mozzarella bocconcini (24 pieces)

½ cup breadcrumbs

1 egg

Recipe continues on next page

......................................................

For the aioli, blend mayonnaise, basil, arugula, lemon juice, garlic, Parmesan, salt, and pepper in a food processor until completely smooth.

In a pan, warm a teaspoon of olive oil on medium heat.

Add the tomatoes and stir to lightly cook and slightly blister their skins. Remove and cool.

In a separate bowl, beat the egg. Dredge the mozzarella in the egg and then in breadcrumbs. Fill the frying pan with olive oil, heat until 400 to 450 degrees, and fry the mozzarella balls approximately 30 seconds each or until golden brown on all sides. Set aside on a paper towel to cool.

Once the mozzarella is at room temperature, use a toothpick or skewer and poke through one tomato then one mozzarella ball, dotting the tops with the basil aioli. Repeat.

# My Bat Mitzvah

Though I was born into a devout Catholic family, I have always been deeply drawn to the Jewish faith. As a kid, I loved how the rabbis spoke to their congregations frankly, without the pomp and frills of the Catholic Church. I loved that there was no such thing as heaven and hell, and I truly enjoyed Jewish music—so much so that I made a mix tape that included both klezmer hits and the entire *Yentl* soundtrack for my Walkman.

Growing up on Long Island, the bar and bat mitzvahs I attended were no ordinary events; these rites of passage were celebrated with an extravagance that befitted the time and place. A few highlights:

- Jimmy Connors sitting at a table signing tennis balls as party favors at one.

- Keith Haring spray-painted Keds sneakers at another.

- The entire Broadway cast of *Phantom of the Opera* performed "Music of the Night" at Lauren Kaplan's bat mitzvah.

- Someone even had Mindy Cohn—Natalie from *The Facts of Life*—as a surprise guest.

Some of the soirees were black-tie, and some went until 1 a.m. For those, you were gifted the Sunday *New York Times* with fresh bagels and lox on your way out the door. There were Academy Award–caliber montages of the b'nai mitzvahs' life, always with the soundtrack of Kenny Roger's "Through the Years" or Paul Anka's "Times of Your Life" playing while pictures of my friends at tennis camp or breakdancing flashed on a screen big enough to light up Times Square.

I had my face painted and my caricature drawn. Videos exist of me singing Samantha Fox's "Naughty Girls Need Love Too," and I amassed enough T-shirts reading, "I Partied at [Insert Name]'s Bat/Bar Mitzvah," to clothe an entire kibbutz.

I'd listen to my friends' mothers fret for months about the big party, how the flowers being flown in from Holland or the elaborate diets they were following to fit into dresses purchased in New York City on the fifth floor of Bergdorf. I think Seth Cohen's mother existed solely on grapes and water for eight whole months before his *Starlight Express*–themed extravaganza. Often an elaborate fireworks show would signal the dessert buffet. One time, a rogue firework blew up the entire challah table, and we had to wait to do the candle-lighting ceremony until the replacement challah arrived. I think you get the point: these folks were not messing around.

One night, I came home from Hebrew school (again, I went by my own desperate choice) really proud that I could recite the entire hoftorah from start to finish—and if I may say, perfectly—with no tutor or rabbi by my side, which most of my friends needed. After my family fell asleep, I remember going into the kitchen and grabbing one pink birthday candle from the drawer in which my mother kept blank greeting cards and odds and ends.

I lit the small pink candle, held it in my hand, and alone, in the middle of our 1980s Formica kitchen, recited the entire hoftorah from start to finish, even closing my eyes at the important parts. When I was done, I blew out the candle and went to bed. The next day was Sunday, and we'd have to get up early for church.

# Mini Italian Challah Grilled Cheese

One of my favorite recipes in which all my worlds collide.

MAKES 1 SANDWICH

2 slices challah bread

1 egg

Pinch of salt, pepper, and oregano

½ cup shaved Parmesan

2 slices fontina cheese

2 slices mozzarella

4 tablespoons olive oil

Heat skillet with olive oil.

Beat egg and add Parmesan cheese with the salt, pepper, and oregano. Coat the two pieces of challah with the egg-cheese wash.

Grill both sides until brown, then add fontina and mozzarella and grill again until melted.

Cut sandwich into 8 individual squares and serve as small bites.

# Playing "Johnny Carson"

One of my favorite games to play with my Papa Charlie was "Johnny Carson."[1] We would take turns being Johnny and the guest. I was usually the guest. More specifically, I was always Charo,[2] and I would stuff my T-shirt with tennis balls and put on my mom's fancy red-sequined bolero jacket, which she wore only once to my cousin's wedding. A tennis racket would serve as my guitar.

My Papa would sit at the elevated counter on our very

--------

1  Let's take a millennial ADD pause. Please Google "Who was Jimmy Fallon before Jimmy Fallon?" and then buy yourself the box set of *The Johnny Carson Show* and watch every episode. While you're at it, also purchase the *The Dean Martin Celebrity Roast*, and this chapter (and probably this entire book) will become more atmospheric.

2  Charo: how to explain. . . You could look her up on *The Love Boat* or maybe just imagine a more ethnically offensive version of Sofia Vergara, with a little vintage Goldie Hawn mixed in for good measure. Little known fact: Charo was an incredibly accomplished Flamenco guitar player.

Long Island kitchen island, light a cigarette, pour himself a J&B scotch and soda with one sugar cube, and announce, "Ladies and gentlemen, my next guest is an exciting young lady who is as uninhibited as she is beautiful! Would you please welcome . . . Charo!" I was ten years old.

On the odd occasion I wasn't Charo or my other favorite character, Liza Minnelli, I was just me, and my Papa would say, "Ladies and gentlemen, introducing one of the pickiest eaters but most adorably foul-mouthed little girls on the planet . . . my Mary." Naturally, I was the only guest he stood up from his desk to greet. Before sitting down, I would address the fake audience first, which consisted of my Grandmother Mary with "the Alzheimer's," who might at that moment be vacuuming the living room rug with her hair dryer. She'd wave to me and then go back to her housework. Before taking a seat, I'd pull the cigarette from my Papa's hand and pretend to take a drag.

When we weren't playing "Johnny Carson," we were brewing coffee so that we could stay up all night to watch the Jerry Lewis telethon, or we were rolling meatballs for the Sunday sauce. We donned captain's hats while we watched *The Love Boat* dock in our favorite place to say out loud, "Puerto Vallarta," and one time, during *Fantasy Island*, he let me dress him up like Zsa Zsa Gabor, complete with blonde wing, lipstick, and a gold lamé hat.

Occasionally, of course, I left his side and, in fact, left the house. I'd return and regale him with tales of where I'd been and what I'd seen, especially if it involved a movie.

He was always game to play along with however I wanted to push the envelope of my overactive imagination. When I told him that I just loved the movie *E. T.* and asked how I could make my bicycle fly, sure enough Papa Charlie would find a pulley and some rope in the garage, tie it to two trees, and by the end of the week, you bet your sweet patootie (as we said on the Carson set), my bicycle was "flying."

The thing is, Papa Charlie and I had this incredibly rich life, with all these adventures, and all of them (at least all the very best ones) took place in two small rooms in my house—in the kitchen or in the den on a sofa in front of the TV.

For their entire lives, my grandparents never traveled, didn't have much money, and lived and worked within the same fifteen-mile radius of where they were born. They moved into our house during the happiest time of my life—my childhood—but the saddest time for them. Papa was diagnosed with kidney failure and was undergoing dialysis, and my Grandma Mary (for whom I was named) was suffering from Alzheimer's disease, so each day we watched her slip further and further away from us. Humor was how I chose to handle Grandma's illness, as the other option was tears. And while their world was closing itself to them, Papa saw that my world was just beginning, and it was going to be, as he'd say, "So big." Weekend after weekend, we traveled without ever going anywhere.

One of my favorite Papa Charlie moments (among many) took place during the Cabbage Patch Kids doll craze. I was desperate like every kid in the 1980s to adopt my very own yarn-haired child, and one day Papa came home from a trip to Brooklyn with a wrapped box. I tore through the plastic wrapping in sheer excitement about what I thought was finally going to be mine. Just as quickly, hot tears streamed down my face when I realized Papa had bought me a knockoff. Taking the handkerchief from his pocket, he said to me, "All the other kids have Cabbage Patch Kids. This is a Brussels Sprout. Now, you're the only kid with a Brussels Sprout."

I still have that doll, but Papa's intent was to make me feel special. I was still the weird girl who hung out with her grandfather too much and pretended to be a coterie of aging television stars from the 1970s, but I was, in a word, special to him. I know Papa would be so proud to know that I actually made it to the real Puerto Vallarta, that I ate real hand-rolled meatballs in Italy, and that I'm at a place in my career where I can travel on a whim. But here's the rub: there will never be a happier place to me than those two rooms, the place marking his exit from the world that he was teaching me to enter.

On that note, I have a strong suspicion that another happy place for me could be on the sofa next to Johnny Carson's—I mean Jimmy Fallon's, desk, and thanks to Papa Charlie, I'm totally prepared.

## Papa's Sweet Scotch and Soda

I was too young to enjoy this cocktail with my grandfather, so he'd place a sugar cube in a glass of club soda for me. After he made his drink, we'd clink glasses and say, "*Cent'anni*" ("May you live a hundred years" in Italian).

MAKES 1 DRINK

1 part J&B scotch

1 part club soda

1 sugar cube

Pour scotch and soda over ice in a rocks glass and then add one sugar cube. Stir until sugar dissolves.

# Hong Kong Flu

Growing up, I had two dads: the real one, whom I saw every day, who woke up, got dressed, kissed us good-bye, went to work, and came home for dinner, day after day; and another dad who lived in newspaper clippings, faded photos, and old records, now bottled up like a genie on a dusty shelf in the basement. That closet was bursting with artifacts from Genie Dad's life: his albums, songwriting books, photos from his performances, wallet-sized black-and-white fan club cards signed by him on the front and listing my mother, Nancy, as his fan club president on the back.

In 1963, my father recorded a record for Chess Records titled *The Hong Kong Flu*. This record, along with many treasures from his storied entertainment past, lived on that dusty shelf, in a closet, tucked away in our basement.

*I'm telling you, you've got the Hong Kong Flu*

*You better stay in bed no matter what you do*

*That's the smartest thing that will help you*

*It starts kind of fast, when your knees feel weak*

*Your temperature rises, all you want to do is sleep*

*But take my advice, whatever you do*

*Look out, look out for that Hong Kong Flu*

My dad was a born performer; there were pictures in the closet of him as early as eight or nine years old, wearing a top hat, performing on stage. When he was in the army, music saved him from being sent to fight in Vietnam when a man named Mike Carubia (who is also a beloved member of the family, as he is known as the man who "saved Dad's life") saw him singing in a bar close to the base and asked him to join the Third Army Band. It was in the army band that he earned the nickname "Rockin Robin."

After the army, he chose to pursue a singing career full-time and headed to California, where he had quick success, landing a deal with Chess Records. He bought a Corvette and started performing up and down the West Coast. I used to imagine him running from gig to gig, like Elvis with his caravan.

He almost got onto *The Johnny Carson Show* with his Chess single, but a week or so before his appearance, there was one recorded US death from the Hong Kong flu, and they canceled his gig.

Disenchanted with the business and California in general, he flew home on a whim and by chance reconnected with my mother, who was staying at his mother's hotel, The Wavecrest. They had met years prior when my dad was Montauk's musical heartthrob and my mom's first kiss (she was thirteen). Older now, and both in relationships, they spent one magical date together and decided that was it.

It sounds like a storybook romance, but that's what really happened. My father promised my mother the sun, moon, and stars and kept that promise. A few years later, my sister was born, and after that, I came along. He moved us into a glass house on a lake (named Lake Success) where the moon would light our living room and the sound of the geese would wake us for breakfast.

We all have inflated visions of our fathers, but mine was extra-extra special and extra-extra puffed up. My dad, in my eyes, was really, actually a star. I would spend countless hours inside the closet, fantasizing about him performing to sold-out crowds, ladies passing out with Beatles-type hysteria for him. Too bad for them, because he only had eyes for my beautiful mother, Nancy, which made him all the more special.

When he played with me, he wasn't Dad; he was Spartacus. I would press his chin in the same spot where Kirk Douglas had a dent in his chin, and he would yell, "I am Spartacus," and lift me into the air with his Spartacus-like strength.

I spent hours of my childhood waxing nostalgic about my father's singing career and the rich entertainer's life I imagined he'd had before us. I spent *much* time pondering whether he was really happy with us or somewhere, deep down, resented us for his choice to become a husband and a father. Did he secretly wish on those boring Sundays spent going to church and tending the lawn that he could drive away in his old Corvette and leave us behind to live that wild life on the road again, chasing his dream, this time hitting it big with no attachments or responsibilities?

The obsession I developed with his former life consumed me, leading me to decide that I too would become a performer. I tried first to be an actress, auditioning, taking acting classes, chasing that dream. If I made it, I'd be picking up where my father left off.

But somewhere between being "almost famous" and becoming a mother, I realized something that made my father seem even more incredible to me—something much bigger than if that closet in the basement had contained a Grammy or multiple platinum records.

During a trip Los Angeles to attend the Golden Globes parties, my perspective began to shift. I had spent the week leading up to the Globes meeting with potential agents at William Morris, United Talent Agency, and Creative Artists Agency. This was *big time*. It was also the time that I learned the concept (to paraphrase—I think it was Parker Posey) of everyone loving you but nobody wanting you. I ended the week by landing an agent but then, after the big meeting where he told me I was going to be a star, never saw or heard from him again.

On the night of the Globes, my girlfriends and I

got dressed up and went to Mr. Chow's in Beverly Hills for a preshow dinner. Dressed to the nines, I was totally uncomfortable in my tight beaded gown and high heels (I hate wearing heels), and I found myself feeling exactly the opposite of what I envisioned; instead of feeling like "the hot ticket" and holding the most coveted invitation in town right in my own fancy evening bag, I was awash with a sadness I could not shake. As my girlfriends giggled about which celebrity they wanted to meet that night, I felt completely detached. The whole everything-and-nothing of the past week felt consuming, and at the precise moment I was about to start weeping into my chicken lettuce cups, I looked over, and Kirk Douglas, the real Spartacus, was at a table with his family, his first outing since suffering a stroke. He was dressed in a tuxedo, sitting in a wheelchair being assisted by a nurse. This did me in. I excused myself from the table, stood outside the restaurant to call my father, and just started crying. I wanted my real Spartacus, the one who chose to leave this world behind to be my dad.

I'll never forget the calm happiness in my dad's voice as I told him much my feet hurt, how soulless Los Angeles felt, and how sad it made me to see Spartacus drink his dinner out of a straw. He told me how he and my mother were at home, snug under a blanket on the couch, waiting to watch the show together—a ritual our family always enjoyed sharing together. A simple "That's Hollywood, kid" and a "Try to enjoy yourself" gave me instant perspective.

My whole life I had thought I would deepen my bond

with my dad when I had finally made it as an actress, but that night I realized that when he said being at home on the couch with my mom was better than rubbing shoulders with all of Hollywood, he meant it. Though I had spent so many dreamy hours wondering if my dad was really happy with his life, he never had. He never felt frustrated or regretful about his "almost famous" alternative life or about leaving his exciting entertainment career for a stable job and the family life.

A few years later, on my dad's seventieth birthday, my parents and my sister and her family came to visit my husband and me at our home in Woodstock. Earlier in the day, in an attempt to surprise him, I took his Chess record to the local radio station and asked the DJ to please play his song and give him a big shout-out for this milestone birthday.

That night, I was so excited to lead him and my mom toward the radio in my kitchen for his big surprise. When the song played, I watched him listen closely. I saw him travel for a moment back to that place, the time that I imagined throughout my childhood was better than us. But when the song was over, he held the hand of the president of his fan club (and his wife of fifty-two years, my mother) and moved very quickly on to what he deemed was a way more important discussion: what we were going to have for dinner.

# Put Your Socks and Your Panties On:
## Life, Love, and Cooking Advice
## from My Mother

My mother, Nancy, exudes a confidence that makes you believe she's an authority on everything. An incredible cook, gift giver, dancer, and joke teller, Nance is always happiest in her kitchen, cooking for her family, and, of course, offering advice. Everything I ever learned about cooking, life, and love I learned from my mother. These lessons were always taught in the kitchen, while she was cooking, which was the perfect venue for her to impart both her culinary skills and her life wisdom to me.

Some highlights:

1. "Always save two meatballs after you fry them, before throwing them into the tomato sauce, for someone you love."

Anyone who knows meatballs knows that these are the two best ones and thus the ultimate sign of affection. Can't tell you how many times my mom slapped our hands when we tried to snag our dad's balls.

2. "A man is attracted to the smell of basil, so use it in everything you cook."

When asked, "Do you think Daddy fell in love and married you because you smelled like basil?" my mother confidently proclaimed, "Yes. Yes, I do."

3. "Put your socks and your panties on."

This was her advice when my sister and I found a mouse living in our house and were afraid to go to sleep, knowing it was on the loose. She advised that if we had our socks and panties on, we would be just fine. I still don't understand what that had to do with anything.

## 4. "Be a wife in public but a girlfriend in the bedroom."

On the night before my wedding, while ironing my veil, she told me that she likes to dance and sing Tina Turner's "Private Dancer" for my dad every once in a while. She then placed the iron down, walked around the ironing board, and went straight into her act for me. I have the video to prove this actually happened or else I wouldn't believe it myself.

## 5. "You can always just whip up a quick frittata."

My mother was always whipping up a "quick frittata" with either last night's leftovers or because someone was stopping by. It was not uncommon to find the painter, our exterminator, or the air conditioner repairman sitting at our kitchen island, taking down one of Nance's "quick frittatas."

## 6. "Don't try cocaine."

Nance would often slip in a quick drug or alcohol lesson while cooking, and it always had to do with something she had "read that morning." "You know, Mary, I read *this morning* about a young girl who tried cocaine at a party, and guess what happened to her? Her head blew up, and she died." In all fairness, her scare tactic worked, and every time I was offered the fancy party drug, I declined for fear of my head exploding.

### 7. "A lady never gets drunk."

Nance doesn't drink. She had one drink (ever), and it was on her honeymoon. If I had a penny for every time I heard about how she lost the use of her knees after that one rum punch and what a gentleman my father was for eating his lobster dinner on the balcony of their hotel room by himself while she lay passed out in bed, I'd be a rich woman.

### 8. "Stay safe. Don't be like those Kennedys. They're just too adventurous."

Nance is a big fan of staying home, as she fears most public transportation. She traveled by airplane only for a short time, enough to show my sister and me a few of the most important wonders of the world, like Disneyland and Boca, but this stopped around 1989, and she hasn't set foot on an airplane since then. She has always used the Kennedy family's tragedies as proof of why everyone should "just stay home." "Who plays football while skiing?" she asked when Michael Kennedy died doing just that, and when JFK Jr.'s plane went down, she didn't need to say a thing; we all knew exactly what she was thinking.

## 9. "*Aglio e olio* can be very comforting."

One time, while home from college for summer break, I was being pursued romantically by a charming but slightly older Italian gentleman. He was from an old-school Italian family and came over to our house one night (on the later side, after a few drinks) to ask my father's permission to date me. As they say in *Goodfellas*, "out of respect." My mother said she felt so badly for him when my father quickly and firmly declined and left the room, like Elvis leaving the building, that she made him a plate of *aglio e olio*, a simple spaghetti with garlic and olive oil. This had to have been around midnight, and they talked until she thought he was okay to leave. She's often made late-night *aglio e olio* to console people.

## 10. "Marry for love and nothing else."

When I was younger, one of my best friends stopped coming to gymnastics with me. Saddened to not see her for our weekly tumbles, I called and asked why. She responded by telling me, "My mother says I'll never meet a rich husband doing gymnastics. She's making me take tennis now." We were ten. When I shared this news with my mother, she sat me down and told me, "Mary, never marry someone for their money or good hair. They can both *go* at any time. Love that's true lasts forever."

I took her advice when I fell madly in love with a long-haired bartender (my husband, Ryan) who looked like Jesus wearing a Phish T-shirt (not my favorite band). I knew I wanted to be challenged and build something from the ground up, that I would require struggle to feel fulfilled. Well, we definitely struggled, but we are still in love. Nance was right. Note: Ryan also has great hair.

And lastly . . .

### 11. "Tell them to cook for themselves."

This is her response every time I call with a stressful story about a high-maintenance celebrity client for whom I am worried about "getting it right." Nance is a great cook, and cooking for others, for occasions big and small, is to her the ultimate sign of affection and love, so she's never really understood why people would hire a caterer to do the job for them. Just a gentle reminder: I am a caterer.

Regarding my celebrity clients, she is far less impressed that these people trust me with their events and far more impressed if they have been on "Kathie Lee." (That's what she calls *The Today Show* hour with Kathie Lee and Hoda Kobe.) A huge Kathie Lee Gifford fan, she took my sister and me many times throughout our childhood to see Kathie Lee and Regis perform, always at the Westbury Music Fair, a venue on Long Island with a rotating stage. You haven't lived until you've seen Regis Philbin sing "Just the Thought of You" while spinning around the room.

## Nance's Meatball Recipe

Remember to save two fried meatballs outside the pot of sauce in a small bowl for someone you love.

SERVES ABOUT 6 TO 8

1 large onion

4 eggs

½ pound beef

½ pound pork

½ pound veal

1 cup Pecorino Romano

1 cup Italian breadcrumbs

4 tablespoons olive oil

6 cups tomato sauce, hot

Dice onions and beat eggs in a large bowl. Add beef, pork, veal, cheese, and breadcrumbs to the bowl.

Roll mixture into palm-sized meatballs.

Heat olive oil in frying pan and add meatballs.

Fry until golden brown, but do not overcook in pan.

Add to a simmering pot of tomato sauce to finish cooking.

# What's a Patagonia?

Recently, I sent an email request to one of the most respected restaurant reviewers in New York City, if not the country, Adam Platt from *New York Magazine*. I was hoping he would participate in an event I was producing titled *Eating Stories*. This idea originated as a one-woman show that I wrote in a mold-infested house in Woodstock one summer with my pal Joanna Adler; it had the working title *If You Can't Join 'Em, Serve 'Em*, inspired by Nora Ephron's play *Love, Loss, and What I Wore*. I adored Nora's play (and everything Nora did) and decided that I would tell *my* stories to sold-out audiences while they were served the food featured in those stories. This was great until I realized that (a) there was a reason my acting career never took off, and (b) I hate being alone. It's way more fun to share the stage with pals than to be by yourself, so, ta da! *If You Can't Join 'Em, Serve 'Em* morphed into *Eating Stories*, which was to feature other food writers and their stories.

I was thrilled when Adam accepted the invite. Adam Platt! When he sent over his bio, I was even more excited to learn that we were both graduates of Georgetown University.

I, the girl with the palate of a twelve-year old, and New York's most respected restaurant critic had something in common.

Eager to inform him of this connection, I responded, gushing, "Excited to share the stage with a fellow Hoya." A Hoya, by the way, is someone who attends or graduates from Georgetown University.

He responded, "I am a reluctant Hoya and fairly certain the only overweight restaurant critic who graduated from the School of Foreign Service."

As the only Hoya who serves hot dogs for a living, I cannot tell you how refreshing it was to receive his email. I never really had the proper language to describe how I felt about my college experience, but from then on I thought of myself as a "reluctant Hoya." When I tell people that I graduated from Georgetown, I get one of two looks: awe or confusion. Awe from strangers aware that Georgetown graduates are known for their big smarts and fancy pedigrees. Confusion from people who have known me for a while. Let's just say, I don't really fit the description of the typical Georgetown student in that I never had any interest in pursuing a career in law or medicine or becoming the next president of the United States.

In fact, I didn't even want to go to Georgetown. I wanted to go directly to New York City to become a comedic actress and writer. My father, however, had different plans for me and bluntly ended the conversation by saying, "New York will always be there. We live twenty-five miles from it. Go get a good liberal arts education. Then if you still have the bug, you can always move to New York." Dad then threw this zinger in: "And I would like you to apply to the nursing school, like your sister, Nanette."

"A nurse? Me?" I asked my father, confused.

"Yes, you're good with helping others. It is a practical degree that you can always use. Just look at how well you take care of Grandma."

(He was right; I did take very good care of my grandmother. But hey, she took care of me. A grandmother with Alzheimer's is pretty amazing about keeping your high school parties under wraps, right?)

I was sure that underneath his tough exterior, he would understand that I had to try to find success acting. He had once been a celebrity himself! Granted, he'd had a hit song about a pandemic flu, but he was a musician with a record deal and swooning fans! Surely he would encourage my dream rather than crush it with a pair of nice, sensible white nursing shoes.

"Nurse first." And that was that. My dad didn't really ask questions; the discussion ended with "You're going."

I remember thinking, fine, nursing. These skills will come in handy if I ever have to play a nurse on a soap opera.

But once I got past going for the unwanted nursing degree, I started to worry about not fitting in at Georgetown. I had spent the first seventeen years of my life not fitting in, trying desperately to be Jewish. I was finally good at it. Those were my people and most of them were going to NYU or BU or other colleges where they could join Alpha Epsilon Phi. Going to nursing school would put me on the same path as people who might as well have been from an entirely different planet: a planet made up of country clubs and cucumber sandwiches with the crusts cut off and Arnold Palmers and ham dinners on Sunday and women who wore dresses emblazoned with palm trees and pineapples and men who wore pastel-colored pants and fuzzy fleece vests. I mean, what's a Patagonia? Even before I arrived, I was panicking. What would I have in common with any of these people?

Enter Annie. I met Annie the first day of freshman year. The minute I laid eyes on Annie, she immediately reinforced my fear that Georgetown was the wrong fit for me.

The day I met her, she was wearing a long, flowy Laura Ashley skirt. I was wearing cut-off jeans and a crop top to show off my "sick abs" and even "sicker" tan. She had attended one of the most prestigious private schools in the country; she had traveled extensively throughout the world before arriving at Georgetown. I went to a public school located on the service road of the Long Island Expressway, and prior to becoming a Hoya, I had traveled to both Orlando *and* Boca. Her bedding was custom made, with monograms and numerous fluffy pillows. My bedding was off-the-shelf Bed in a Bag. When she spoke, her enunciation was perfect. When she wrote, her penmanship was the finest. She had custom stationery, again, monogrammed, on which she would write thank-you notes the hour after she was gifted something. When I spoke, things like "My dawg's name is Candy, and I love cawffe" slid awkwardly off my tongue, and when I sent my thank-you notes . . . Who am I kidding? I never sent thank-you notes.

Two girls, who on the surface had nothing in common, bonded over one simple thing: our deep love of a great laugh.

It was as simple as that. Annie was and is the funniest person I have ever met in person, and we became inseparable based on our ability to crack each other up, to make endless prank phone calls, and to do really good (and really bad) celebrity impressions. I have notebooks filled with funny short stories that Annie and I wrote during classes instead of the European civilization or abnormal psychology notes they should contain. I've treasured our friendship since day one, and I've always regarded my love for Annie as a living, breathing testament to "you never know." You never know who will end up being the Laverne to your Shirley, the Amy Poehler to your Tina Fey.

Annie convinced me to come clean to my dad about my complete lack of interest in nursing, to have the courage to tell him that this was not to be my life's work, and encouraged me to change my major to English.

Yes, like my new pal Adam, I too was a reluctant Hoya. But Georgetown and Annie and all those deserving

Georgetown students with whom I had nothing in common, well, they inspired me. And every time I start to poke fun at myself because I serve crab cakes at my Georgetown classmate Bradley Cooper's parties for a living instead of eating crab cakes as a guest at his parties, I remind myself that it was the not-exactly-small chip on my shoulder that propelled me through my doubts and insecurities to go on to make my life and my business conform to exactly what I wanted. And guess what? That fancy university, from which I often joke I graduated magna cum party, invited me (at Annie's prodding) to speak on campus as a published author. Going back twenty years later, with my unlikely pal by my side, I thought to myself that maybe I belonged after all.

Now, about those pants with the sailboats: that's some kind of inside joke, right?

## Mini Turkey Club Tomato Cups

Annie was the first person to invite me to a fancy country club, and let me tell you, it was the best turkey club I ever had. These bites go perfectly with an Arnold Palmer (½ lemonade, ½ iced tea). For a little extra fun, add some vodka, and for even more fun, wear a dress with a palm tree on it.

MAKES 24 PIECES

**1 pint cherry tomatoes**
(in certain seasons you can find heirlooms,
which I love for both the color and the flavors)

**½ pound roasted turkey, diced small**

**6 pieces bacon, fried and crumbled**

**5–6 large leaves iceberg lettuce, diced small**

**2 tablespoons mayo**
(you can replace the mayo with a simple oil and vinegar)

**Salt and pepper**

Cut off the tops of the tomatoes and scoop out the pulp, then rinse, drain, and set on a dish towel to dry.

In a bowl, combine the turkey, bacon, and lettuce with mayo or oil and vinegar. Add salt and pepper for flavor.

Fill cherry tomatoes with mixture.

Set on tray and serve.

# Italian Hot Dogs

During my junior year of college, by the skin of my teeth, I got a spot in a study-abroad program living with eighteen other very lucky *studenti* in a gigantic villa in Italy. I didn't get into the villa program initially, as my grades were not as exceptional as those of the other students, which included my four best girlfriends. Hating the thought of being left behind, I stopped into the admissions office to plead my case, begging them to find a spot for me, promising to work harder on my Italian, even vowing to watch every single Fellini movie.

And it worked, because a month before my gal pals were about to depart for Europe, leaving behind a small Italian girl with no posse, a spot opened up and was offered to me. *Buon viaggio*, I was off to Italy.

Food, wine, and Italian cinema were part of our

curriculum. We had a cook named Clara who prepared the most incredible Italian meals every night—she made hands down the best *penne quattro formaggi* on the planet. Sitting high above the city of Florence in an exclusive hillside town called Fiesole, the Villa le Balze was donated by the Rockefellers to Georgetown University so that students could immerse themselves in Italian cuisine and history. Think of it: one of America's premiere philanthropic families donating a villa—an entire villa—to their beloved alma mater so that students could expand their minds and palates in one of the most beautiful and delicious regions of the world. Days would be spent in our beautiful classroom located in the grotto area of the gardens. We only had classes Monday through Thursday, so weekends were spent on the Eurorail traveling to other beautiful locations.

I'm not the greatest traveler, as we weren't really a family who left home too often. Actually, as much I wanted to go along with my friends, I was terrified to leave the United States, and my family, for any significant period, to say nothing about the distance. Since my mother always equated travel with death, saying goodbye at the airport was as tearful as Italian goodbyes could be. My father had to basically pry me off his leg to get me on the plane. My mother was too torn up to even accompany him to the airport.

I boarded my first international flight and ended up sitting next to what felt like an entire platoon of the German army, with whom I drank and played cards with for the entire flight. The first thing I did when we arrived at the airport in Rome was throw up in the bathroom. Lucky for me, my four best girlfriends were much better traveled, possessing the proper footwear, maps, and travel guides. I was the definition of an accidental tourist . . . which also happens to be one of my favorite William Hurt movies.

I spent almost six months living and traveling with my gang, and to be honest, I always felt like the fifth wheel—not as adventurous or worldly or, quite frankly, as excited as they were to move around Europe as much we did. They were constantly sharing items with me that I forgot to pack, pushing me to join them, and urging me to stop being *so* excited there was a McDonald's in Rome.

Toward the end of the semester, I wanted to give them a special thank-you for putting up with me, my homesickness, and my resistance to full Italian immersion, so I came up with an idea.

Borrowing a garden cart from the maintenance shed and lugging it up the very steep hill from the villa into the small town of Fiesole, I purchased all the beer and hot dogs the *supermercado* supplied. Cart filled, I rolled it all the way back down the very steep hill (dropped a few Heinekens) into the award-winning Villa le Balze gardens and threw what I'm sure was the only hot dog and beer party overlooking the city of Florence. I'm sure this is *not* what the Rockefellers had in mind when they donated their family villa to Georgetown in the name of culture.

It was my gift to my friends, and I think they were grateful for a little taste of home, because after six months of eating pasta, there is such a thing as too much carbonara.

When I returned the cart to the elderly gardener the next morning, he uttered something in Italian and smiled. I had no idea what he said, as my Italian was pretty terrible, but I've always pretended it was "In all the years I've worked here, I've never seen such a simple yet special gathering done so elegantly and with such panache. You will go on to do great things, young Italian America lady, who often speaks to me in some sort of Italian-Spanish hybrid that includes way too many hand gestures."

*Fine.*

## Italian Pigs in a Blanket

These are my beloved cocktail wieners with a Euro 'do.

MAKES 24 TO 30 PIECES

1 pound Italian chicken sausage

4 tablespoons pesto, plus more for serving

2 sheets puff pastry thawed in refrigerator

2 eggs for egg wash

1 teaspoon each of oregano, garlic powder,
and grated Parmesan cheese, stirred together

..............................................

Preheat oven to 350°F.

Place the chicken sausage in a small baking pan to keep the links straight and pack in snug to prevent them from curling while they cook.

Bake for about 12 to 15 minutes until the sausage is cooked through and set. Remove from the oven and cool (this can be done a day in advance).

Place a sheet of puff pastry on a lightly flour-dusted cutting board. Cut the ends off the chicken sausages and line them up end to end across the long edge of the pastry. Spread a thin line of pesto along the edge of the sausage onto the pastry.

Roll the dough over the sausage, cut the puff pastry, and egg wash the seam where the pastry will reach the other side to seal the dough together. Repeat with the remaining links and refrigerate or freeze until ready to bake.

Once chilled and ready to bake, cut the pigs into approximately 1-inch pieces and place on a parchment-lined sheet tray. Brush the tops with egg wash and sprinkle with the oregano mixture. Bake for approximately 20 minutes, rotating the tray halfway through.

Place on serving tray and serve with additional pesto.

## PART II:

# CIGARETTES

## "THINGS ARE GOING TO START HAPPENING FOR ME NOW."

—Navin Johnson, in *The Jerk*, upon seeing his name printed in the phone book for the first time

# One Christopher Street

"I think we're done here, Robbie," my mother announced to my father once she finished unpacking the entire contents of my kitchen cupboard, which at the time included two dishes, a fondue pot, two soup bowls, and her M-O-M mug. Eager to begin their not-so-long twenty-five-mile journey back home, my father threw on his coat, placed a wad of about $300 in my hand, warned me to stay away from drug addicts, and—*click*—the heavy prewar metal door slammed shut behind them.

I was alone for the first time, in my own Manhattan apartment. I had waited exactly twenty-one years and four months to hear that door close. Alone, just me and my five hundred square feet of paradise located on the corner of Christopher Street and Sixth Avenue on the ninth floor with an amazing view of Pieces gay bar, Gray's Papaya, and The

Bagel Buffet. Since I had an affinity for all these thing—bagels, hot dogs, and gays (in no particular order)—I took this as a sign that I was home.

In the middle of the apartment was a Murphy bed. For those of you unfamiliar with them, a Murphy bed is a bed that you pull down from the wall for sleeping and push up to store when not slumbering. I must have raised and lowered that bed fifty times that first night, fantasizing about all the other people who had slept in this unique wall bed before me. Mostly, I pondered whether I had the discipline to both make my bed and lift it back into the wall each morning.

The plan—I think "deal" is the better word—I made with my dad was that he would pay my first two months' rent but after that, I was on my own. If I could not come up with the rent at the end of my paid-for grace period, I would have to either move back home or take in one of my cousins as a roommate. Beyond confident that I could become the next Gilda Radner over the next sixty days, I shook his hand and accepted his terms.

Soon after my parent's departure, I concluded that I was far too lazy to commit to a relationship with the Murphy bed, so instead I set my mattress on the floor in the middle of the apartment. Once the sheets and pillows were perfectly arranged, I sat on my windowsill and lit my first cigarette in my own apartment. It remains, to this day, the best cigarette I would ever smoke. I then poured myself a glass of white wine and drew myself a bath. These were all very adult things that I imagined one with her own Manhattan address would do.

Once I was bathed and buzzed, my first gentleman caller arrived. Oh, I wish it had been as torrid as it sounds. A serial monogamist, I've had three boyfriends in my life: one in high school, one in college, and one who became my husband. The visitor was my boyfriend Ryan, whom I had been dating at that time for almost five months. Ryan had long brown hair, hazel eyes, and a goatee. The first time I asked my father what he thought of Ryan, he looked up from his newspaper, took a sip of espresso, and responded, "He looks like Jesus." I was so excited for Ryan to see my fancy new apartment because, well, it was fancy, and his was—how do I say this politely?—not. His was located on the Lower East Side across from the famous Meow Mix lesbian bar, which provided a great place for me to wait for him in bad weather. Nothing like watching a bartender light her nipples on fire as you pout because your boyfriend is running an hour late.

His apartment was slanted, as in, if you dropped a ball or a quarter, it would roll all the way across the room. His room was a paper-maché'd—or as Ryan would correct me, *sheet-rocked*—cube in the center of the living space. He had two roommates, one kind and one deranged. The kind one would tiptoe past the paper-and-water-mixed cube on his way to the bathroom. The deranged one would throw stuff like a piece of fried chicken or boxes of condoms into the cube as we slept, since the walls on this lovely sleep box didn't go all the way up to the ceiling. I'm not even going to describe the bathroom. Just imagine Port Authority meets the bathroom of a Grateful Dead show at Nassau Coliseum, if the door hit your legs while you were peeing.

Back to my fancy apartment. "What do you think?" I asked Ryan as I gave him a tour of my new place with the pride Henry Hill's girlfriend, Janice, in *Goodfellas* took in showing off her new digs, proudly exclaiming as she pointed to each piece of furniture, "It's all Maurice Villency." I proudly showed him that the apartment had two walk-in closets, a dining alcove with a window, and a view of Gray's Papaya. I think this feature excited me the most.

After the tour, it started to snow, the most beautiful city snow I'd ever seen, or maybe the first city snow I'd ever seen. Snowflakes as big as matzoh balls were illuminated by the flashing rainbow lights coming from Pieces gay bar. We headed out and ate dinner at a corner restaurant called Le Deux Gamins. We drank wine, watched the snow, shared our big, big dreams, and declared with absolute confidence that we would both make it in the city. I was going to be a famous actress, and he was going to be an even more famous photographer.

After dinner, we stopped at Marie's Crisis. Stop the presses: I now lived down the street from a place where a group of mostly gay men would gather and sing show tunes around a piano? Heaven was for real! I pulled out a great version of "Maybe" from *Annie*, Ryan threw a few dollars in the tip jar, and then we went next door to Arthur's Tavern, where we danced to the music of Sweet Georgia Brown until 3 a.m. Sweaty and drunk on vodka sodas, young love, freedom, and endless possibility, we walked home in the snow. We said good night to both my doormen and giggled at how small the elevator feels when you are drunk and have an elevator attendant.

Before we passed out, I asked Ryan to please move my mattress from the floor onto the Murphy bed. I decided that I could handle both the city and this bed that I'd store in my wall. I had no idea how I was going to do it, but I knew with certainty that I would. I closed my eyes, and as an ambulance screamed up Sixth Avenue, suddenly twenty-five miles felt so far away. New York was now my home.

# The Captain and Tennille

The year Ryan moved into my apartment, we went to a street fair in Chinatown and purchased two illegal baby turtles. We named them "The Captain" and "Tennille" after the popular 1970s superstar singing duo "Captain" Daryl Dragon and Cathryn Antoinette "Toni" Tennille. Their big hits "Do That to Me One More Time" and "Love Will Keep Us Together" often filled our small Christopher Street apartment.

For many years, The Captain and Tennille swam harmoniously, side by side. Their love was total and pure and a daily reminder to us to make time to deepen our affection for one another. They started out in a small round bowl. We kept them above a hutch, which housed our one ginormous computer, which we would fight to use. As our lives upgraded, so did theirs. We moved to a nicer place; they got a fancier tank. Our tastes would change, and suddenly their rounded

Zen rock garden bowl became a sleek mid-century modern rectangular tank furnished with pink neon rocks and white plastic trees. Their bond was a part of our daily lives.

For years we left each other little love notes, not from us but from the Captain to Tennille, or vice versa.

Dear Captain [I would write],

You truly rocked my shell last night. Thank you for that wild swim. I look forward to doing it to you "one more time" this evening.

Please, remember, my precious, to pick up a pack of Pall Malls and some Dubonnet [we were convinced they drank things like Dubonnet and Frangelico on the rocks] because when you get home, my baked Alaska will be on fire for you!

Love,
Tennille

Dear Tennille [Ryan would reply],

No problem, my precious Toni. Make sure you're wearing that powder-blue negligee that I love so much when I arrive home, the one with the white furry pom-pom cape and the white furry pom-pom slippers. You know how that drives Daddy crazy.

Love,
Your Captain

PS: Did you drink all the chardonnay again?

This went on for almost ten years, our turtle love notes piling up. In our notes back and forth, the Captain and Tennille traveled to Pennsylvania's Mount Airy Lodge and chuckled about their romps in the heart-shaped hot tub. They ate a lot of raclette, and contemplated adoption but concluded that Tennille was far too lazy to mother. They were learning Italian together for their upcoming trip to Venice.

Life was good for the turtles, until one day, with no warning, The Captain murdered Tennille. For ten bliss-filled years, they were the very picture of a happy couple, until one day, we could only assume, The Captain finally grew tired of hearing Toni sing "Muskrat Love" and ate her. Not just a quick "chop" in whatever place in a turtle's anatomy would kill her quickly and painlessly—no. The Captain killed her with the violence of ten years of slow-simmering rage, as if she ate the turtle pellet he was eyeing just one too many times, and he snapped. I'll spare you the details, but poor, poor Tennille.

We were in shock. They had been our fondue-loving, record-listening (with shared headphones), tantric sex turtles for most of our relationship. I removed what was left of Tennille from the tank. I placed her in a white shoe box, drew a black crucifix on it with a Sharpie, and placed her in the freezer next to a bottle of vodka and package of frozen spinach. Obviously Tennille needed a proper funeral, so we stored her in the freezer until our next trip upstate, when we decided a fitting tribute would be to give her a streamside burial.

On the side of the road, on the way to our small farmhouse, we tossed her from a wooden bridge and cranked "You Light Up My Life" by Debby Boone on our car radio as we watched her frozen shell sink to the bottom of the river.

Our obsession with their love affair now became a murder mystery. We became completely focused on knowing what set The Captain off. Why this day? Why not any other day of the ten previous years in which they had lived in wedded turtle bliss? I no longer wanted The Captain in our home, so instead of sending him to Rikers, where he belonged, I sentenced him to Ryan's office at our catering company. To me, The Captain was no longer the gentleman turtle who wore dickies, thoughtfully lit candles, and fashioned tapestries and sheepskin pillows into a love nest for his Tennille before they made love. To me, The Captain now was a murderer and a confirmed bachelor. He became Jeffrey MacDonald, the ex–Green Beret who had killed his family in the 1970s and, before the bodies were even cold, quickly got a new young girlfriend and a boat called *The Recovery Room*, which he kept in Marina Del Rey.

The honeymoon was over. The notes stopped. The Captain grew larger, the fantasies were shattered, and more often than not, we shunted the responsibility for his care onto our various coworkers. He's still alive, by the way, still living in our office, swimming around a very dirty tank, older, maybe bitter, or maybe happy as a . . . turtle.

# Careful What You Wish For

For a short while, I took a pitstop in my career journey and accepted a job at the Make-A-Wish Foundation. My job title was "wish granter." My only job responsibility was to make wishes come true.

I first called Make-A-Wish on a lark, bursting into tears during the hold music, giving me even more reason to hide behind a tissue box in my cubicle. I was working at a talent-management agency, which was a disaster of a job, and I had reached the point of no return.

On that day, as on other days in the agency, I was wearing full receptionist headgear with earphones and a microphone, and I knew I had to keep the call short and sweet as my boss would be returning soon from her two-hour lunch at Café des Artistes with a wicked buzz and an appetite for more spite than normal. The agency did in fact represent some of the biggest and brightest names in show business—a fantastic opportunity for someone who wanted to be a manager someday but a terrible place for someone who was actually trying to become one of those bright shiny clients.

Life back then went like this: I'd run from audition to audition, and by audition I mean, stand in line half the day with other unrepresented actors talking about how Bill or Al or Sharon just got two lines on a *Law & Order* episode. Doors continued to slam in my face, one after another. I bravely recalled, again and again, how James Lipton once said to me after my failed audition for the Actors Studio that Sally Field tried out nine times before she was accepted there. On the days I wasn't facing painful rejection, I was working at the agency, stuffing endless envelopes with Maggie Gyllenhaal's headshot or photos of other actresses my age, putting forth their names for film roles that I would have cut off my pinkie toe to get.

My morning routine was first to make coffee while waiting for the photocopier to finish printing the day's breakdowns, which were daily casting notices from big studios that I would assemble and staple and place on each of the five managers' desks before they arrived at work. It was impossible for me not to read every page while multitasking, resulting in what my bosses always dubbed VBC—very bad coffee—all the while fantasizing about the managers sending me out for these parts.

"UNTITLED HBO project looking for MEADOW SOPRANO, 18–21, Caucasian, female, Italian American.

Meadow is Tony's (the Mob Boss) daughter who is caught between childhood innocence of loving her father and learning what her father does for a living." This one in particular rocked me: I *was* Meadow! What more did they want, my grandma's meatball recipe and a letter from the nuns? When I mustered up the courage to ask my horrible boss if I could submit my headshot, she laughed viciously and sent me on an errand—something really important, like purchasing a raincoat for her dog.

Every day, as I placed the breakdowns on their desks, I hoped and prayed that this would be the day the managers would see in me something truly special. Something that would make them say, "Take off that headgear, Mary. Your time has come! Go straight to *Saturday Night Live.* Do not pass Go!" But sadly, no matter how many subtle hints I dropped, along with some not so subtle hints and maybe even pleas (confession: I couldn't help myself and submitted my home-made headshot—taken of myself by myself—for the role of Meadow Soprano), they never saw anything more in me than just Mary, the assistant who made really bad coffee.

I was done. I was defeated. It was time for change. So off to Make-A-Wish I went. Making dreams come true for the most deserving children in the world seemed to be a significant step up from where I was.

While I was working at Make-A-Wish, we held our annual fund-raiser at Christie's Auction House. Our fund-raisers were joyful celebrations of the work we did mixed with gut-wrenching sadness that made everyone with a beating heart dig deep into their pockets for these kids. The Wish Kids were—and remain to this day—my greatest teachers. I will never forget watching one of the boy's faces when he entered the lobby of Christie's, which had been painted in bright, vibrant colors by Sol Lewitt. This child was one of my favorite Wish Kids. He was six but an old soul, exceptionally personable, with a smile that made Sol Lewitt's colors fade in comparison. He came over to give me a hug and asked me if he could use my cell phone to call his grandmother. I handed him the phone and listened as he said, "Grandma, I'm at Chris-pies. You would love how beautiful it is." He then hung up, thanked me for my phone, and chased an hors d'oeuvre tray across the room.

While I was prepping for the event, I met a young intern named Lydia Fenet. Lydia was tall and elegant. She was perfectly dressed from head to toe in fancy designer clothes, including a pastel Hermès scarf wrapped perfectly around her neck. She was a Christie's girl, straight from the pages of *Town & Country* magazine. One of those girls who went to fancy boarding schools, had great handbags, and lived in glamorous apartments with the right address. She had a confidence unusual for someone our age. I was intimidated and hesitant to even introduce myself, never mind ask her for help finding extra tables for the event. I took a deep breath, told her my name, and confessed to having no idea what I was doing. Lydia smiled and responded, "Me neither. Let's go look."

During our search for tables, we became immediate

friends, and almost twenty years later, she remains one my closest friends and favorite dream collaborators.

The Christie's event was a success in many ways—not only because I had met Lydia, but because the job forced me to look at where I was in my life and where I was going. I realized that I wasn't done chasing my dream of being an actor. So after three years with Make-A-Wish, I swallowed hard and said, "Try to be a star, take two."

This time, though, I had another strategy. I answered an ad in the *New York Times* that read, "Upscale boutique catering firm seeks temporary employee to work with art, fashion, and entertainment clients." Perfect! I could make some money but still go on auditions.

I arrived at Fifth Street between Second and Third Avenues for my job interview at DM Cuisine, bright-eyed and eager, wearing a a colorful "adult" blouse I borrowed from my mom. The office was tiny but sweet, and I was feeling fairly confident about snagging the job when in walked the boss, Chef Daniel. He was all business, seemed distracted, and kept his comments and questions brief and rapid-fire. Had I worked in catering? Could I place a rental order? One positive of my acting career is that if someone asks me if I can do something, I say yes with utter confidence, even when I have no idea what I am agreeing to. How hard could a rental order be?

How many glasses would you order for a party of one hundred? Apparently "one hundred" was the wrong answer. If you had a thirty-inch round table, what size cloth would you put on it? Shit! Tablecloths? Round tables? What happened to the "entertainment" part advertised with the job?

Hoping to steer the conversation away from tablecloths, I assured him I could polish up my rental knowledge, that I learned fast and could contribute a great book of clients. That got his attention.

Yes? Daniel was now interested. Like who?

I began naming a bunch of fancy people I had read about in *Town & Country* or seen in *Hamptons Magazine*.

"Well, you can learn the rental side of things, and if you can bring in business then we have a place for you here, but only for three months. If you don't bring in business, then you can't stay." He said this like he would be revoking my admission to Harvard, not rescinding a sales job at a catering company. On that note, I was hired and started at a salary of $50,000. This was the largest amount of money anyone had ever offered me for work in my life. And with that I shook his hand and began my role as Mary Giuliani, catering sales rep.

Here are some highlights:

- Day 1: A disgruntled coworker throws a bunch of files on my desk, says, "Here you go," and ignores me for the rest of the week.

- Week 1: I call my mom not one but ten times asking questions like "What's a samovar?" or "Does the fork go on the right or the left?"

- Week 2. Day 1: I placed my first rental order for a party at Conan O'Brien's apartment. When no glasses and ill-fitted tablecloths arrive, I learn how good I am at running in heels down Fifth Avenue to Crate & Barrel.

- Week 4, Day 1: I book a party but mark it on the calendar on the wrong day of the week—my first angry client and an even angrier Daniel.

- Week 4, Day 2: I get fired.

- Week 4, Day 3: I grovel and get rehired.

- Weeks 5 to 12: I get really good at online Scrabble and send out exactly one press kit to the only fancy person I know who could possibly afford our catering services: Lydia, my poised new friend from Christie's.

- Week 12, Day 1: 9 a.m.: I get fired for real.

Half an hour later, while I was cleaning out my desk, right as I was about to walk down the street to hand Daniel my keys and cross "catering sales rep" off my list of careers, the office phone rang. It was Lydia calling from Christie's to say how much she enjoyed meeting me, and how nice our press kit was, and how perfect the timing was as Christie's was looking for a new exclusive caterer. She had no *idea* how perfect the timing was.

I was treading water, trying to figure out my next move, growing more nervous about what would happen if I really did lose this job while becoming frantic about my stalled, or never really started, acting career. Lydia's call was like a message, a sign that it was time to take something seriously.

Life comes down to moments, and while I had no idea then what the "it" was, I knew it was something. Her call was a wakeup call about the dreams you think you need to fulfill and the dreams you don't realize are swirling around in your subconscious. Yes, it was a shift in plans. Yes, it was not exactly what I had envisioned. But you know what? It was just what the doctor ordered. I realized that finally—*finally*—I was about to step into one of the greatest roles of my life.

# Lunch with Bob

I've never won an award. Not one medal, trophy, distinguished mention, or yearbook superlative like "Most likely to cure Zika." And I always think that one of the main reasons is because I never committed to anything long enough to be rewarded for my efforts.

A few examples:

- Brownies: I stopped going after two weeks as I did not exhibit Brownie-like behavior. Never even saw one green sock from the Girl Scouts, let alone a rainbow badge.

- Nursery school: My mom said I took one trip down the slide, ate a cookie, grabbed her hand, and said, "Take me home. I finished." I wouldn't go back for a year.

- Gymnastics, soccer, softball, tennis: I signed up for all but rarely showed up for any.

So while my parents will never ask me to come home to clean my trophies out of their basement, I have something that I think is even better: not one but three voicemails saved on my phone from Robert De Niro.

Right after college, I enrolled at Upright Citizens Brigade (UCB for my fellow comedy nerds) to pursue my lifelong dream of becoming a cast member on *Saturday Night Live*. I think I was two classes in when I found out that my friend Pete got a job as the Cue Card Guy at *SNL*, so instead of learning how to "embrace my ensemble" or "take responsible risks" with my fellow improv classmates, I'd ditch class to visit Pete on the *SNL* set, positive that direct contact with Lorne Michaels, via Pete and his cue card pal Wally, and not my incredible comedic timing would seal my fate as a future cast member.

Pete the Cue Card Guy invited me to the *SNL* set often to watch him write big words in black and purple markers on large white poster boards, and if this wasn't just the greatest thing ever, he went one step further and dropped on me the most coveted of invites. He told me he could sneak me in the back door to the *SNL* after-party on the night that Robert De Niro was hosting.

"Yes, Pete. I'd love to attend the *SNL* after-party," I responded, as if I had been waiting for this moment my entire life. "Can I bring my sister?" I'm fairly certain he said no, but I brought her anyway. This was a huge rite of passage, and I needed a family member present to both share it with me and serve as witness in case I passed out from the shock of meeting Robert De Niro in person.

My sister and I arrived at America's in Chelsea. The place was naturally packed to the rafters. Looking back, of course, it had to be, and that makes our earlier obsessing over our outfits even more hilarious—as if anyone would be looking at us. The photo of us from that night, dressed to kill, still occupies a prominent spot in my parents' living room years later. I can't imagine how many cosmos it took for my sister to approve my outfit—a fedora and a brown sweater with a pink felt dog on it. But that's not really the point.

The room was the comedic purgatory I hope to see when I die. Dan Aykroyd holding court at his table with—wait for it, fellow *SNL* geeks—Laraine Newman. Lorne Michaels sipping on a martini. Jimmy Fallon buzzing around the room, and there in the center of the room, there he was: my Bob.

"There's no place for us to sit," my sister nervously informed me, clutching her cosmo for dear life. I scanned the room, and she was right. All the tables were loaded, and it quickly became obvious that we were simply two hangers-on snuck in the back door by Pete the Cue Card Guy. I couldn't let this night be a failure, so I dragged Nanette over to the only table in the entire packed restaurant that was open: right next to De Niro's.

"Mary! We can't sit here!" She turned around a small white sign sitting on the table that read, "Reserved for Harvey Keitel." With confidence sponsored by Ketel One Vodka, I looked at my sister and hissed, "Just sit down!" We lasted about eight minutes until other misfits (probably those invited by the grips guys) made their way over to the table. We welcomed our fellow F-listers with open arms.

De Niro was literally inches away, and who knew when we'd actually get kicked out of these seats? "You have to say something to him," slurred my ninety-eight-pound sister, who now had more cocktail bravado than Belushi on a bender. So I did the unthinkable: I tapped Robert De Niro on his shoulder. "Excuse me, Mr. De Niro?" Reminder: I was wearing a fedora and a sweater with a pink felt dog on it.

"Um . . . Bob."

"Um . . . Bob," I repeated and said, "We both have houses on one of the most beautiful beaches in the world."

I sat there sweating as he went through a catalog in his mind of his real estate portfolio. Thankfully, he looked at me and said, "Montauk?"

Ding ding! "Yes, Montauk." I went on to tell him my very quick family history of Montauk, and I held his interest for north of three minutes, south of five, until he asked, "What's your name?"

"Mary Giuliani."

And with that, he turned his back on me and went back to the guests at his table.

"He hates Rudy!" I reported back to my sister. Things had been going swimmingly until I mentioned my last name; it was not the first time I had been mistaken for a member of the mayoral family. I had blown it with Bob. Dejected, I told her it was time to go. My moment with Bob was gone.

We stayed at the table for maybe ten more minutes when I noticed Bob and his entourage getting up to leave. Lyrics from the Milli Vanilli song began to play in the soundtrack of my mind. "It's a tragedy for me to see the dream is over."

On his way out, he stopped at our table, put out his hand, and asked, "Do you have a card?"

I stared, open-mouthed and motionless. Thank God for my sister, as she whipped into her purse and grabbed one of my business cards and wrote "MONTAUK" on the back with a black pen, handing it to him as he walked away.

We screamed with excitement and ran to the bathroom to call our parents to tell them we had just pulled off an Italian miracle. "Who died!?" my mother answered the phone, jolted awake at 3 a.m. as we squealed in her ear and babbled our story.

We danced ourselves home to our apartments in Murray Hill and both vomited until the sun came up. All in all, it was a wonderful night.

Three months later, I was sitting at my desk at my catering job, and Victoria, the receptionist—and also the woman who would sage our office after a party gone wrong—told me a woman named Robin was calling from "Bob De Niro's office."

Barely composing myself, I picked up the phone. "Hi Mary. This is Robin from Bob's office. He met you at a *Saturday Night Live* party and he would like to have coffee with you. Are you available sometime over the next few weeks, and do you have a cell number I can share with him?"

Luckily for me, I had just gotten a cell phone (a StarTAC—the fancy kind) and was able to share my suddenly very open calendar and (now highly coveted) 917 cell phone number. We hung up, and I screamed: I told the whole office, then called everyone I knew, including my sister, who screamed just as loud as I did.

Now, let's take a moment to pause and discuss how a normal person would process this call. Here are a few options:

- "Wow, that's pretty cool. I'm going to have coffee with Robert De Niro. Perhaps he is interested in having a party catered."

- "Wow, that's pretty cool. I wonder if he wants to talk to me about something in Montauk, since I shared with him my love of and connection to the town."

- "Wow, that's pretty cool. Maybe he wants to cater a party in Montauk and naturally thought of me. How flattering."

But normal is something that other people do.

I decided—with almost no hesitation—that my time had finally come. I was being discovered. This was the moment. I didn't need to finish my semester at UCB. This was simple math. I wanted to be an actress. The universe placed me at a table next to the greatest living actor of our time, and now I was going to be cast in his next film, in the role of his daughter. The *New York Times* would call it a cinematic masterpiece and label me his muse, and the work we would create together would become as important as *The Godfather II*. I, Mary Lucille Giuliani, would save Bob De Niro from making *Dirty Grandpa*.

So I waited. And waited. And waited. Until three weeks later, I had a message on my cell from a blocked number: "Umm, Mary. This is ummmm Bob."

It took three voicemails from blocked numbers (which I shared with anyone who would listen, including my dry cleaner and my dentist) for us to finally make a date to meet.

On the day of the dreamed-of coffee date, I wore a pink shirt with butterflies, which perfectly described what I had going on in my stomach. I entered the restaurant (nearly empty), and the maître d' didn't even ask my name or whom I was meeting, just welcomed me by ushering me to the back room of the restaurant, which was even emptier. He sat me at a banquette and asked me if I needed anything.

About fifteen minutes later, I heard footsteps. I looked up, and there he was. He was every character I've ever loved all wrapped up in one perfect package. The *Once Upon a Time in America* Bob, the Vito Corleone Bob, and the Jimmy Conway Bob from that scene in *Goodfellas* where he takes a drag of his cigarette while "Sunshine of Your Love" by Cream is playing.

"I'm sorry, I'm late . . . Excuse me, I have to take this." He answered his cell phone. This was when I observed for the first time that he had not one but two cell phones.

I'd never seen that before. *Mental note: get another cell phone; people will think I'm important.*

He came back.

"Where do you live?" was the first question. About sixty-three other questions soon followed.

"Where do you work?"

"What do your parents do?"

"Where did you go to college?"

"What does your husband do?"

"What did you study?"

"Tell me about Montauk."

Short of revealing my blood type and Social Security number, I gave him everything. In between the questions, we managed to fit in a glass of chardonnay, a Caesar salad, and an espresso.

After I had nothing else to give, he asked for the check, told me how nice our time together had been, and got up and walked out.

I was not used to being left at banquettes. I guess he could see the disappointment in my eyes, because no sooner had he left our table than he turned around, walked back over to me, and asked, "Are you okay?"

I wasn't. In the seconds that passed between his good-bye and his return, I had realized that I would not be playing his daughter in the greatest film of his career. I would not be invited to Sunday dinner at his house. And I would not get that small kiss on my cheek with a "You're the greatest, doll" like I'd hoped. When I look back now, I find his question not arrogant but sincere, as it showed me he was aware of his impact and wanted to be kind.

"Yes. I think. Can I just ask you one question?"

"Sure."

"What made you call me and want to meet?"

And this, my friends, is the one thing I am not going to share. Because some things in life should remain sacred, and also because I love intrigue. Come on. I love that we still don't know what Bill Murray whispered into Scarlett Johansson's ear in *Lost in Translation*.

I will say that it was kind and innocent and made me feel so very special.

So what happened next? Not a damn thing. I didn't see him again for another two years, until I was catering a party for the Tribeca Film Festival. I caught a glimpse of him from the corner of my eye and was sure I was long forgotten. I walked by him to clear a glass, and he reached out, touched my arm, and said, "Mary, good to see you!" I was shocked that he remembered my name, but before I had time to respond, he was bombarded with people.

The same thing happened four years later. I was catering a party for my fellow Georgetown classmate (and actual pal and muse of De Niro) Bradley Cooper. Again, Bob arrived, and I was sure he had forgotten me. While I was replenishing a nut tray, we made eye contact, and he said, "Mary, nice to see you." Before I could respond, Heather Graham arrived and started chatting him up.

Three years later, I was walking down the beach in

Montauk with my friend Grace, and who do we see exactly where the ocean meets the shore? Yup. Bob. Grace spotted him first, and I, as usual now, grew nervous that he had forgotten me.

"Mary, nice to see you!"

We made very quick small talk before two of his friends joined him on the beach and we got the feeling we should keep walking.

And that's it! That's all I got.

I know: it's not a fireworks ending. Really long story for what? Here's the what (or at least what I think is the what): We expect that all big stories have a big finale and that the result of meeting someone of this magnitude no doubt will be a life changer. But the thing is, as small and silly as it may sound, it *was* a life changer, a confidence boost of the greatest kind. And this is the biggest lesson my career has taught me. Not everything has to be big. Not everything has to be skywriting. Finding the big in the small works for me and allows me to be happy with what I've got. If we all want more from something, aren't we always going to be disappointed? "Making it," I've come to realize, is all relative.

So, while I still haven't won a trophy or earned a bee-keeping badge from the Girl Scouts, Robert De Niro knows my name. And guess what? Sometimes, that's enough.

# Mini Caesar Salad Rolls

**These go perfectly with a glass of chardonnay.**

MAKES 24 PIECES

### DRESSING

1 small garlic clove

Kosher salt

2 large egg yolks

2 tablespoons fresh lemon juice

3/4 teaspoon Dijon mustard

2 tablespoons olive oil

3 tablespoons Parmesan cheese

### SPRING ROLLS

8 (8.5-inch) rice paper rounds

8 ounces Romaine lettuce, leaves finely chopped

Recipe continues on next page

......................................................

Whisk dressing ingredients together and season with salt and freshly ground pepper.

Mix the lettuce with a small amount of dressing, just enough to barely coat the leaves. Place in a bowl to the side.

Pour some warm water into a large shallow dish. Submerge one rice paper round in water until it begins to soften, about 45 seconds. Place on a sheet of parchment paper. Place a small amount of lettuce in the center of the rice paper. Tightly roll into a cylinder, enclosing the lettuce. Repeat with the remaining rounds. Cover with a dampened paper towel or wrap in plastic. Chill. Can be made 4 hours ahead.

When ready to serve, remove from plastic and cut each roll into 2-inch-long pieces. Stand upright on a platter and top with a spot of dressing. You can put crumbled pancetta, Parmesan cheese, or chopped nuts on top for flavor and garnish.

# Suddenly I See

Do you agree with me that the best part of a movie is the visual montage passage? Do you know what I'm talking about? It's the part of the film when a really great song plays while the lead character goes through some type of personal transformation. At the beginning of the song, she has a bad haircut and cannot properly cook an egg, but by the end, she is strutting down Fifth Avenue in a sassy dress with great new haircut and has mastered classic French cooking, surpassing Julia Child with her beef bourguignon.

If I were teaching a film class, I would cite these two wonderful films as perfect case studies of the visual montage: *Baby Boom* and *The Devil Wears Prada*. (Other great examples include *Tootsie*, *About Last Night*, *Karate Kid*, *Can't Buy Me Love* . . . I could go on.)

First, *Baby Boom*, featuring "Coming Around Again" by

Carly Simon: Diane Keaton's character, power executive JC Wiatt, is left a toddler named Elizabeth in a distant cousin's will. Possessing not a whit of motherly skills, JC struggles to fasten diapers and even tries to coat-check cherubic Elizabeth at the Four Seasons when she has an important business meeting. By the time the song is over, however, JC has mastered the art of mothering, gotten Elizabeth into a fancy NYC private school, and decided to leave her high-stress career for a simple life in the country, all in the name of maternal love. This movie is *so* good that it even provides you with a second song montage when she begins her baby apple sauce empire, growing it from one jar to millions in sales by falling back on her business savvy. (This ditty is more of a 1980s David Foster instrumental sax kind of number.)

Next, in *The Devil Wears Prada*, "Suddenly I See" by KT Tunstall is the background for a total transformation of Andy (played by Anne Hathaway). She walks into the Condé Nast building in a terribly unchic Ann Taylor pantsuit with an outdated haircut, no makeup, and bad eyebrows and by the end knows how to flawlessly handle her hideous boss, Miranda (a brilliant Meryl Streep), and has undergone the perfect *Vogue* makeover. It is during this song that Andy has her "aha!" moment and realizes this fancy fashion career that she once eschewed is now the path she wishes to pursue.

If I had to pick a part of my life to set to music for my montage moment, it would be my time working at DM Cuisine under the guidance of chef and owner Daniel Mattrocce. Playing in the background would definitely be

Diana Ross's "I'm Coming Out!"

When I arrived at DM Cuisine, I was very young and very green. I had only taken the job to help pay the bills and pass time before I earned a cast spot on *SNL*. I never saw the job as anything more than yet another stopping point in my journey to fame and knew very little about catering or fine dining in general.

Daniel was the consummate professional and perfectionist. He had studied fine pastry in Paris and worked at The Plaza during the time when working at The Plaza was a really big deal. He never took shortcuts, and he worked harder than anyone I had ever met. When he wasn't in his kitchen whites, he was impeccably dressed, donning signature fancy bow ties and perfectly pressed shirts from Paul Smith. He lived on one of the toniest blocks in Manhattan and had the dreamiest country estate, which he had spent years decorating to perfection. Daniel hardly spoke to me for the first three months I worked at DM. If he did, he was curt and distracted. He had no real interest in getting close to me, as I'm sure I was one of many who came and went, promising to bring him big business but ultimately disappointing him.

It was only after Lydia called from Christie's that Daniel asked me to accompany him on a trip to visit a client. He was much more comfortable in the kitchen, and while clients loved him, he preferred the company of a good chicken stock or a hearty lump of puff pastry to a face-to-face with Manhattan's elite.

I was so nervous on our cab ride from the East Village to the Upper East Side. This was before cell phones, so you actually had to talk to the person sitting next to you rather than pass the time by googling "Is Chita Rivera her real name?" Small talk also was not Daniel's thing, which only made me fill the cab with nervous chatter. I asked him lots of questions, and he replied with one-word answers. His one request was that I take notes while we met with the client. "You are just here to observe," he reminded me. He did not say another word. When we arrived at what was then the largest private residence I had ever seen in Manhattan, he turned into Mr. Rainbows and Sunshine, smiling and almost singing to the doorman, "Helloooooooo, we're here to see Mrs. *X*" (think big!).

I stood behind him as we were escorted into a living room so large that you could have landed a 747 on the coffee table and watched him greet the housekeeper and Mrs. *X*'s assistant with total admiration and respect, even making a little joke about the last time he had been there and his failed *croquembouche* (a word I would need to look up after we left. I looked up a lot of terms that year, including *samovar*, *French service*, *tarte Tatin*, and *langoustine*).

In walks Mrs. *X* and, wow, was she dressed to kill, head to toe in designer duds, flawless. She loved Daniel and greeted him as if he were the single most important meeting of her day, and since I'm not sure she worked, maybe he was. She barely even said hello to me, which made me very self-conscious of my clothes and demeanor, particularly my (gulp) Ann Taylor pantsuit.

When they started to talk business, I reached into my purse and pulled out a large yellow legal pad that I had grabbed from the office. I got a steady flow of death stares from Daniel as I started to jot down words like *Atkins*, *lavender lemonade*, and *Chilean sea bass*. With no idea why I was on the receiving end of the evil stares, I kept writing. The meeting went on, and when they air-kissed goodbye, Daniel didn't say a word to me for the whole elevator ride down. Once out of the lobby and onto the street, he announced we would be making one stop. We walked and walked and walked and walked, him not saying a word, me not asking where we were going.

When we arrived at Bergdorf Goodman, I was excited and confused. Were we going shopping? Were we getting facials? Was he dropping me off so I could apply for a job? I was impressed with how well he knew his way around the store, ushering us up to the seventh floor very quickly with a "This ain't my first rodeo" attitude. This was my first visit to the seventh floor of Bergdorf, which houses the finest in home furnishings, tabletop design, stationery, and children's layettes and an exquisite café filled with Ladies Who Lunch. Straight to the stationery counter we went. He was greeted with familiar hellos by every sales person on the floor, some even calling him by name and kissing him on both cheeks. He asked for help with leather-bound notebooks, and I nearly died to see the price tag on the one he chose. Purchase made, less than ten minutes later, we were back on the elevator and deposited onto the street. Daniel hailed a cab to take us back to the East Village. In the cab, somewhere between 49th and 48th Streets (outside the entrance of Christie's), he handed me the bag from Bergdorf containing the hunter green leather Smythson notebook. "This is what you use when you take notes on a client visit." I was both reprimanded and rewarded, a common theme in our relationship.

This passing of the fancy notebook marked a turning point for me in his catering business. I didn't stop messing up—on the contrary, I made so many rental mistakes that a special sales rep was assigned to me at the rental company to proof my orders (thanks, Anne McDermott), and failed to know a single thing about many of the fancy foods we were serving. One time he called me into the kitchen to ask me what I meant when I simply wrote "salmon" on a menu order for a client. I was confused by his question, so I responded, "Salmon." To which he angrily replied, "Which kind?" I had no idea. So he then showed me how to prepare poached, smoked, and baked salmon. He taught me which accompaniments went perfectly with caviar (a food I had never tried or even seen—he even forced me to taste it in front of him and laughed when I spit it into a cocktail napkin) and how to caramelize a baked brie. A few times I even assisted him with a breakfast prep at 4 a.m., an hour when I was usually just returning home to pass out, not waking up to work.

The notebook meant, without his saying it, that he was

ready to invest the time and money into making me good at my job. It would be up to me whether to take him up on the opportunity to learn or to squander it when something shinier came along. And little by little it worked.

With Daniel I had to work, I mean really work. He was the first person who didn't allow me to use charm to get away with murder; he let me be all Sicilian and quit in a dramatic flourish but then reconsider when my cooler head prevailed (I actually did quit twice and came back both times). He was my officer, and I was his gentleman.

Slowly but surely, I found myself wanting to do better for Daniel and for me. And as I got better at the business, I started to fall in love with the concept of a hard day's work, business hours that had no start or stop time, and the *ta da!*—the reward for a job done well. I could make people happy in the same way a good performer makes an audience happy, except *I* could dream, plan, and execute this show. I didn't have to wait for it; it was there for *me* to create.

Daniel showed me that nothing about the business was going to be easy in the same way that nothing about becoming an actress was going to be easy, the difference being that I actually possessed talent for event planning. Before our eyes, I traded one dream for another and committed to this new one—the one I hadn't asked for. I was going to become a caterer. Period.

If great mentors do their job well (and well was the only way Daniel did anything), there comes a time when the wings they have helped their protégés strengthen start to flap. At this, my "visual montage" moment, when my hair was perfect, I had ditched the Ann Taylor pantsuit, and I knew the difference between poached and baked salmon, I made the most difficult professional decision I've ever made to date—and flew away from Daniel. We didn't talk for many years. I reached out a few times with no response, and then thankfully one day, years down the road, he agreed to meet me for lunch.

I sat across the table from him, older, more accomplished, with a deeper understanding of why he had taken his time before getting close back then, of the sacrifices he had made to earn the success that he did. I started by saying that I was sorry—sorry if I had hurt him by leaving, sorry I hadn't realized how much that could hurt (I had since been burned badly by two employees who left me to do their own thing). And his response was so elegant and so perfectly Daniel. "There was nothing I could ever do to stop you from becoming what you needed to be." There he was, teaching me yet another lesson: to drop the bitterness. As a business owner, colleague to colleague.

Daniel taught me that people will leave, people will hurt you, people will move on, but if you've done your job well—and by "well," I mean helped them find their wings—then all you can feel is proud when it's their turn to fly.

# Colin Cowie and My Joan Rivers Earrings

I have a million questions running through my head every day that mostly pertain to my career. Why am I doing this? Is this the best job for me? Is this it? What's next? Did they like it? Do they like me? At what age does one start Botox? Was the chicken cooked properly? But I've pondered one random, ongoing conundrum for years: did Mrs. Garrett from *The Facts of Life* really love those girls, or was it just a job?

This is my head and the dizzying questions that plague it.

However, there have been moments in my career when I have allowed myself to stop, not question what's next, be in the moment, and take it in. To be "in my zone," as I learned on a trip to Kripalu Yoga Center (my twice-a-year rehab), means to be doing what you love. Lucky for me, a very handsome gentleman from South Africa showed me the way to my zone.

While working at DM Cuisine, I received a call from Colin Cowie's office asking us to cater an event for Elizabeth Taylor with *InStyle* at Christie's. Those are four very fancy names in one sentence, and I was *ready*. However, if Liz's signature color was violet, mine was green, because that is exactly what I was. Novice doesn't even come close.

I had only been a catering sales representative for a short time, and still barely knew the difference between a salad fork and an entrée fork, but a moment revealed itself to me in this opportunity, and it was up to me, and me alone, to figure out what to do with it. Armed with my fancy new notebook and my Joan Rivers earrings (my mom has a terrible QVC problem; I'm certain my inheritance is located in a storage container in Paramus filled to the brim with key pieces from the Joan Rivers, Susan Lucci, and Tova Borgnine collections), I was off to Christie's for the big planning meeting.

When I opened the boardroom doors at Christie's, I could not believe what I was seeing. The room was filled with top-level Christie's executives, the whole executive team from *InStyle* magazine, and a team of Elizabeth Taylor's most trusted handlers.

We were all awaiting the arrival of Colin Cowie. And then, as if a Hollywood director had yelled out, "Action!" the boardroom doors flew open.

Colin did not walk, he sauntered. He entered the room

with his team, dressed perfectly and lint-lessly in black. When he spoke, his accent was foreign and sounded like the most beautiful music I had ever heard. He made words like *over budget* and *overtime* sound like sexual positions you were dying to try. This man was the closest thing to James Bond I'd ever seen. To this day, I'm convinced that he could fix you a martini dusted in gold with one hand while disarming a bomb with the other, but of course, as he would tell you, "only if the lighting plan was perfect."

I looked around, observing this room filled with accomplished high-level executives, my heart racing with that "please don't call on me, please don't call on me" feeling.

When lavender carpets, crystals, elephants (yes, elephants), Nehru jackets for the men responsible for picking up the elephant poop, lighting, sound, press, and VIP guests were checked off the to-do lists, Colin looked at me and introduced himself.

"Colin Cowie," he said as he shook my trembling hand. "And you are?"

"Mary Giuliani. I'm the caterer."

"Mary Giuliani," he repeated. My name had never sounded more beautiful.

He then gave me what I call "My Education with Colin."

"Food is like theater, darling: we must make our best impression in the first act; if we don't, we lose our audience! We dine with our eyes, darling!" With a small wink he began, "The trays are to be covered with moss, the pea soup must be topped with chervil, the caviar must be Petrossian."

When someone in the room suggested we serve pigs in a blanket (Elizabeth Taylor's favorite—and mine), he quickly retorted, "I'm only serving pigs in a blanket, darlings, if they are presented in mounds of caviar."

I loved this man. If the Beatles had the Maharishi, I had Colin Cowie.

I think he could see the fear in my eyes, because he paused, walked over to me, and said, "I have total confidence in you, darling, that you and your team can pull this off."

The man who threw Oprah's five-day fiftieth-birthday bash, the man who could transform a tennis court into the inside of a royal palace with a snap of his fingers—he had confidence in me, a girl who faked a learning disability in an attempt to get out of taking high school Spanish.

But that vote of confidence was all I needed. I worked extra hard to make sure everything was perfect for that event. I wanted Colin to notice me, even tried to make my Long Island accent sound a bit more South African. In the theater of my mind, he was Bob Fosse and this encounter was an audition for *Chicago*.

When the event day arrived, I was determined to make sure that we did the best job we could, and even when Elizabeth Taylor arrived two hours late because she had inadvertently locked herself inside her hotel bathroom, I made sure we had enough food and drinks to keep the guests happy until she appeared.

I observed Colin throughout the entire project, how he presented himself, the pride he took in what he did. He was an artist, and each event space was his canvas. His craft was less about serving others and more about transformation, creating something magical, taking guests to a faraway land. While Daniel may have turned on the lightbulb in my new career, Colin walked me right into what would become my dream.

And when that party was done and my lint-less Maharishi sauntered off into the night, I knew exactly what I was going to do: start my own business. Three years later, Mary Giuliani Catering & Events was born.

## Fancy Pigs

We never did serve pigs in a blanket in mounds of caviar for Elizabeth Taylor as Colin suggested, but here's an idea that might have worked.

MAKES 24 MINI CUPS

Nonstick pan spray

2 pounds thin-cut bacon, strips cut in half

1 small tin Petrossian caviar

½ cup crème fraîche

.......................................................

Preheat the oven to 350°F. Turn a mini muffin pan upside down and lightly coat the bottom with nonstick pan spray.

Crisscross 3 slices of bacon over each upturned mini muffin cup, creating a small cup, and then place another mini muffin pan on top so that the bacon slices are compressed between the two.

Place the pans on a rimmed baking sheet and bake until the bacon cups are crisp and browned, about 20 minutes.

Remove the baking sheets from the oven and set aside to cool completely.

Lift off the top pan.

Carefully remove the bacon cups from the bottom pan and place them on a paper-towel-lined baking sheet to drain, upside down.

Fill with dollop of crème fraîche and top with Petrossian caviar.

# Am I a Foodie?

"I'm so nervous to invite you over for dinner, Mary. What could I possibly cook for you?"

This happens more often than not, and to be honest, as my catering company's profile has grown, invites to home-cooked meals have become few and far between. Since no one loves a dinner invite more than I do, and I fear I've "party-experted" myself into social pariah status, I feel I must come clean and fess up about my true relationship with food.

Let me begin: I am not, nor have I ever been, a foodie. I'm also not a chef. And while I love to cook, thankfully for my clients I do not cook the food for my catering company. I leave that up to the pros.

"No, Mary, I didn't breastfeed you," my mother has told me. "I tried once, and you didn't like it."

Once?

She followed that up with, "Mary, you just didn't like my milk, so I gave you soy formula." She then confessed that after sustaining my life on soy formula for a full year, she realized that I was actually allergic to soy, so she just started to feed me pizza because I didn't like anything else she tried. I was one year old.

My first memories of eating socially take place in the Notre Dame Elementary School cafeteria, where I would sit with a bunch of kids who actually ate real food, things like sandwiches, chips, apple slices, and milk. But not me. I would pull out a triangular tin-foil-wrapped piece of room temperature pizza that my mom would warm in the toaster oven at the same time she was making my chocolate chip pancakes (the only breakfast I would eat), pack it in my *E.T.* lunchbox, and off I would go. I ate pizza for lunch every day except Mondays, when I would pull out a meatball hero made from Sunday supper leftovers.

Sick of getting made fun of for my delicious foil-wrapped Italian delicacies, I convinced my mom that I was now allergic to the smells in the lunch room: you know, that weird bologna-and-milk stench. She felt terrible for me, so for a while she would meet me during recess and slip me my pizza through the playground fence with all the stealth of a drug dealer.

Fish? I don't eat fish.

"What!?

"Not lobster or shrimp?"

"You grew up in Montauk and don't eat fish?"

I am asked these questions with wide eyes, confusion, and slight disdain every time I'm pushed to confess this piece of info. And I have to be pushed because it's a fact I'm not proud of. Why no fish? Simple.

My grandfather used to take me to the fishermen's docks in Montauk when I was a little girl, always on what felt like the hottest and smelliest days of the year. We'd get out of his smoke-filled Caddy, and he'd stomp out his Kent and acknowledge the fetid odor by yelling, "Morning, ladies." If that didn't kill my desire to order clams on the half shell, the flies swarming around the popped-out eyeballs and fish intestines that lay rotting in the hot sun did. This is why I don't eat fish. My husband, Ryan, can occasionally get me to eat raw tuna, but I must have first completed at least three sake bombs and the tuna must be swimming in soy sauce. Mario Batali got me to eat an oyster once, but it was fried, we were in New Orleans, and I was so drunk it could have been a duck's uterus and I wouldn't have known the difference.

I'll take a time out to acknowledge the fact that I grew up in a house with not one, not two, but three amazing Italian cooks and that my mother made real home-cooked meals six nights of the week. Thankfully for Nance, just like the Lord, she got one day off, Friday, when we ordered pizza! If you're still with me, my childhood meals entailed pizza for lunch at school and also every Friday night. Oh, wait, there was also the beef tea. When told by my pediatrician that I was anemic, my mother boiled pieces of beef until it morphed into a chunky, oily broth called beef tea, and she would chase me around the house and watch me until I drank every last sip. It was disgusting.

College: much of the same. I ate Domino's once a day and brunched at Taco Bell. I once applied for a credit card from the Republic Bank of North Dakota (with a 40 percent interest rate) just so I could rack up a bill at Wisemiller's Deli in Georgetown for my morning bacon-egg-and-cheeses and nightly grilled cheeses or chicken sandwiches. College is also where my beverage history begins. Since I didn't drink much in high school, I felt I needed a sophisticated drink to call my own. The first night of freshman year, at Champions Bar on M Street with my roommate Joanna, I looked up at the bar rack, saw a glowing green liquid, and declared that the Midori Sour was going to be "my thing." I spent half of my freshman year throwing up neon green in various bathrooms around DC.

After college, I lived on Gray's Papaya hot dogs (because they cost a quarter) and tequila until I stepped into the fancy catering offices of DM Cuisine. This is where my true education in food began.

I knew nothing about catering, let alone the rules of high-society catering. My mind was blown when I realized that people on Park Avenue actually have two kitchens: one for show, one for the caterer. While at DM Cuisine, I planned event after event for the top 1 percent of the 1 percent, serving these five things:

- Smoked salmon wrapped in dilled crepes

- Vegetable timbale

- Cobb salad (one socialite swore it was "her thing" and asked for a tasting prior to the lunch so she could dictate the blue-cheese-to-diced-ham ratio)

- Chilean sea bass

- Tarte Tatin with vanilla ice cream

No matter where I went, up and down Park and Fifth Avenues, clients always requested the same menu. I served so much sea bass on the Upper East Side from 2000 to 2005 that I may be single-handedly responsible for this beloved fishy's aquatic shortage.

In 2005, desperate to stop selling sea bass and serving food on silver trays, I decided to start my own business. But the food and the serving style were going to be my own. I remember writing the first hors d'oeuvres list for my catering company:

- Pigs in a blanket

- Mini grilled cheese sandwiches

- Mini burgers and fries

- Mini Philly cheesesteaks

- Grandma Mary's mac and cheese

You get the point. I then swore off silver trays for good and created trays out of wood, Lucite, and anything colorful. Ultimately the vibe I was going for was what Laurie Colwin describes as "nursery food" in her cult memoir *Home Cooking*, food you would only see on the kids' menu. I had decided that I would only serve that kind of food.

By 2006, I had done it. My crowning achievement that year was looking into a packed party and watching Carolina Herrera chow down on one of my mini grilled cheese sandwiches with fontina, surrounded by pieces from that season's clothing line. A heaping tray of pigs in a blanket caught the attention of the CEO of J. Crew, Mickey Drexler, which led to twelve years of business and friendship, and my mini buffalo chicken grilled cheese blew Ina Garten's hair back so much that she invited me to come on her show and cook them with her.

So, what do I eat now? Much of the same, except these days I slip the occasional green juice in there, just to stay alive. The tequila is less frequent. I occasionally allow some broccoli and kale to infiltrate my plate.

And what does my daughter eat? Pizza and hot dogs. Karma.

# Wisemiller's Chicken Madness

A few years ago, the Cooking Channel cracked the code for the sandwich that put me into credit card debt. I've adapted their recipe to be served as party-sized bites. I encourage you to visit Wisemiller's if you're visiting Georgetown, or make this at home. This sandwich will change your life.

### MAKES 4 SANDWICHES OR 32 MINI BITES

6 slices thick-cut bacon

¼ cup olive oil

2 boneless, skinless chicken breasts (about 1½ pounds)

1 large yellow onion, peeled, cut into ½-inch rounds

Kosher salt and freshly ground black pepper

1 green bell pepper, sliced ¼-inch thick

1 red bell pepper, sliced ¼-inch thick

½ teaspoon garlic powder

¼ – ½ teaspoon cayenne powder, to taste

8 slices provolone

¼ cup mayonnaise

8 slices white bread

¼ head iceberg lettuce, shredded (about 2 cups)

2 plum tomatoes, thinly sliced

Potato chips, for serving

Pickle spears, for serving

......................................................

Preheat the oven to 400°F.

Lay the bacon in a single layer on a rimmed baking sheet and bake until crisp, turning once, about 15 minutes. Drain on a paper-towel-lined plate. When cooled slightly, crumble the bacon into bite-sized pieces. Reserve 1 tablespoon of the bacon fat from the pan.

Heat a two-burner stove-top grill pan on medium/medium-high heat. Oil the pan with 3 tablespoons of the olive oil.

Liberally sprinkle both sides of the chicken breasts and onion rounds with salt and pepper.

Carefully lay the chicken down on one end of the grill pan and the onions on the other.

Cook the onions until charred on both sides and slightly softened, 6 to 8 minutes. Transfer to a cutting board. Cook the chicken until charred on both sides and an instant-read thermometer inserted into the thickest part of the breasts registers 160°F, 18 to 20 minutes. Transfer to a cutting board. Rest the chicken for 5 minutes. Dice the chicken into ½-inch pieces and cut the onion into large bite-sized pieces.

Recipe continues on next page

Add the remaining tablespoon of olive oil and reserved bacon fat to a large sauté pan on medium-high heat. Add peppers to the pan. Season liberally with salt and pepper. Cook, stirring occasionally, until the peppers start to brown around the edges and soften slightly, 2 to 4 minutes. Add the grilled chicken, grilled onion, garlic powder, and cayenne to the pan. Stir to combine and cook, stirring occasionally, until the chicken and onion are warmed through, 1 to 2 minutes.

Shingle the cheese on top of the chicken and vegetables, turn off the heat, and cover the pan until the cheese is just melted, 2 to 3 minutes.

To assemble, spread 1 tablespoon of the mayonnaise on both halves of each slice of bread. Place ½ cup of the shredded lettuce, 4 to 5 slices of tomatoes, and one-quarter of the chicken mixture on half of the slices. Sprinkle the crumbled bacon evenly among the sandwiches, and top with remaining bread.

Cut each sandwich into 8 small pieces. You may need a toothpick to keep all the ingredients together.

Serve immediately with potato chips and pickle spears.

# Strippers Eat
# Hors d'Oeuvres, Too

The one rule that I knew about starting a catering business, especially one without customers, is that you never turn down a party, even when you get a call to cater a birthday party for a stripper. Strippers, you see, have birthdays, too.

The stripper-wife (who was incredibly nice, by the way) informed me that the theme of the party was "Naughty Carnival." Her only food requests were Jell-O shots and cotton candy margaritas. If I ever imagined that I'd be catering a party with stripper poles, it was when I envisioned the "utter failure" scenario: something that I'd be forced to do on my way down, not as an early gig or resume builder.

I remember calling my mom (which I do about six times a day).

"Hi, Ma."

"Oh, hi, Mary. You know, I was thinking. Don't you think you and Ryan should be starting a family instead of a business? If you worked a little less, I know you would get pregnant."

"What are you talking about, Mom? We already started the business, and things are going great! In fact, we just booked our first five-figure party."

"That's great. Who is it for?"

"Ummm . . . a very fancy stripper and her very wealthy husband."

"Mary, just remember two things; Daddy and I love you no matter what you do, and there is always an extra room in the basement if you and Ryan ever want to live with us again. Oh, do you need new pots? Wolfgang Puck is coming up at 3 p.m." (My mother's QVC habit is very real.)

I decided I had to change my attitude toward this party. I mean, how often was I going to get to cater an upscale Naughty Carnival? Armed with this inspiration, I started to get excited. I sat down with my small team for a brainstorming session. First I thought of a Ferris wheel—we would serve mac and cheese in cones from the wheel—and from there the ideas kept pouring out. Fancy corn dogs, caramel bacon popcorn, and mini fried Oreos rounded out the menu.

Inappropriate though it was, the party was held in an old synagogue on the Lower East Side. This was not exactly the place for "Trixie" to be flaunting her ta-tas! The room was lit like a red-light district, the bar had two sexy ice luges under which guests would assume the position for shots, and there was a stage with three stripper poles set on mirrored platforms.

Hours in, the party was happening; the Ferris wheel was a huge hit. There were more shot glasses than beads at Mardi Gras, and I received several high fives from my fancy stripper. Just when I was about to take my first grand creative catering bow, the event planner came running over to me and handed me a spray bottle and a rag.

"Mary, the performances are about to start. Your waiters have to wipe down the stripper pole with this special solution after each dance!" I looked over at the shirtless waiters (client's request) and knew there was no way I could bring myself to humiliate them further by asking them to wipe down stripper poles all night. I didn't know what to do.

Life comes down to moments, right? Well, this was my company, and I was now the captain of the ship. If the ship went down, I was going to be the last one on it, and dammit, those poles would be cleaned!

Once the stripper-wife completed her first dance, I dutifully ran out with my rag and spray bottle. Sadly, I'm not as graceful as those ball girls at Wimbledon, and I was wearing a short little dress, so you can imagine how unsexy my maintenance act was as I tried to avoid crouching at the wrong angle over the mirrored platform. I must have gone back and forth from my Ferris wheel to that pole ten times before I caught my reflection in the mirror. Instead of my face, I saw my father's looking back up at me, saying, "Mary,

Zig Ziglar[3] once said, 'If you learn from defeat, then you haven't really lost!'"

The only thing I learned was that I never wanted to work at a strip club. At the end of the night, I took my spray bottle and my rag and grabbed the first cab I could, hightailing it outta that tarnished temple. Turns out Naughty Carnival life just wasn't for me.

---

3  Zig Ziglar is a self-help guru my father often quotes.

# Cotton Candy Margaritas

**They sound gross, but I have to admit, they taste pretty good.**

MAKES 1 DRINK

.............................

2 parts tequila

1 part fresh lime juice

1 part triple sec

1 package of cotton candy

.....................................................

Fill glass with cotton candy.

In separate shaker, fill with ice and combine the rest of the ingredients, shake, and pour over the cotton candy.

## Mini Corn Dogs

MAKES 24 MINI CORN DOGS

1 cup yellow cornmeal

1¼ cups all-purpose flour

½ teaspoon salt

⅛ teaspoon black pepper

¼ cup sugar

3 teaspoons baking powder

2 large eggs

1 cup milk

1 quart vegetable oil for frying

1 (16-ounce) package cocktail-sized beef frankfurters

36 wooden skewer forks, 3–4 inches long

......................................................

In a medium bowl, combine cornmeal, flour, salt, pepper, sugar, and baking powder. In a separate bowl, gently whisk the eggs with the milk and stir into the dry mix.

Preheat the oil in a deep saucepan or mini fryer to 350°F.

Insert wooden skewers through the center of each frankfurter.

Dry frankfurters with a towel, then dust with cornstarch and shake off the excess. Then hold the frankfurters by the end of the skewer and dip in the batter until well coated. Let the excess batter drip off.

Carefully holding the end of the skewer, let the corn dogs fry for 5 seconds before letting go to prevent them sticking to the bottom of the pot. Fry until lightly browned, about 3 minutes. Drain on paper towels.

# Harry Potter

I don't know of any other person who has gone straight from strippers to Harry Potter, but that was exactly my trajectory.

We had been in business for all of about two months when I received a call from a very prominent—actually the best—event planner out of Los Angeles (known in the industry as the Black Widow, as she left a wake of destroyed florists, caters, and valet parkers whose careers she'd crushed when they'd disappointed her). She had attended a party I did the previous month and must have been impressed, because she was calling to ask me to cater the Harry Potter premiere.

Hogwarts and Quidditch: this was big time! On the call, she shared that the party was for fifteen hundred attendees (!!!) and asked me whether I thought I could handle it. "Sure thing!" I said with the breezy confidence of someone in business for all of two months, hung up, and began what was to become a month-long panic attack leading up to the premiere. I wanted to be an in-demand caterer? Well, here was my chance.

When you are a caterer hired by an event producer, the event producer is the boss. She speaks for the client and shares the vision with you. Ultimately, you do everything you can to execute the client's vision, even if you disagree with it. The first order: the waiters should be "Potteresque"—specifically, women who looked like witches. The older and frailer the better.

Now, imagine trying to get twenty septuagenarian "witchy" women waiters to carry fifteen-pound chaffing dishes, filled to the brim with food, or huge trays loaded up with champagne. A special casting call would be required for this gig. At the interviews, we asked applicants if they would be comfortable with "physical labor." My favorite moment was when one potential witch didn't hear the question correctly, thought I asked for her physician's number, and took out a small phonebook and asked me, "Which one?"

I was in trouble. Even if these witchy waiters could lift the trays, it would take them hours to walk from the kitchen to the buffet! As the planning process went on, the Black Widow shut down most of my suggestions that deviated from her master plan. The event appeared doomed. In Potter-speak, maybe cursed?

In the month leading up to the party, my life was 24/7 Harry Potter. I was determined that every single thing we did for this party would be perfectly Potter. I should also note that at the time I said yes to this event, we had exactly one full-time employee and were delivering parties not out of a fancy catering truck but out of my Jeep Cherokee, which had my college sticker in the back window. Ten to twelve trips were sometimes required to get everything we needed to one jobsite.

The day of setup, I arrived and approached the Black Widow. The first thing I noticed was that her staff was mostly male. I'm not sure if she read my mind, but she saw me sizing up her crew and said, "Mary, I don't hire that many women anymore. They cry too much. I hope you're not a crier."

I took a large gulp and said, "Me? Nope." I then walked away and burst into tears.

Setup went smoothly, and the party began. In my head-piece, I heard the Black Widow hiss, "Mary! Drinks! Now!" which was my signal to send in the witches. I took one look at the room filled with fifteen hundred guests (including celebs, New York VIPs, studio heads, and the entire cast of the Harry Potter film) and then at my assembled army of old witches lining up to grab their trays. Then I did what every successful new business owner would do: I had a complete and total breakdown. Panic-stricken, I ran down to the bathrooms, turned off my earpiece, locked myself in a stall, and stayed there for the first hour of the party, praying to God that all would go well.

But instead of God answering my prayers, I heard the

voice of my patron saint, Colin Cowie, whispering in my ear. "Mary, why are you hiding?"

"I'm scared, Colin. The old ladies are going to die, or even worse, spill an entire Gobletini in the lap of a Warner Bros. executive. We don't have enough food. How will we ever turn over the VIP room into a disco in time for dessert? The Black Widow is going to destroy my reputation; my company will close; my dreams will be shattered, and I'll have to go back to answering phones and wearing a headset for a living."

"Darling," Saint Cowie purred, "A black widow is a simply an insect. You must own this moment. I will never forget the time the Sultan of Kashmir instructed me to ride an Arabian horse into the desert and wait for three days for a goat to appear, which would lead me to a rare lotus flower. From that I would extract the third petal to give me the last perfect ingredient for our specialty cocktail."

Saint Cowie began to command me as if I were Moses receiving the tablets. "This is your moment! Get on your Arabian horse, grab the reins, and take control of this party. Face your fears!"

"Th-th-thank you, Colin," I stammered. I unlocked the bathroom stall and reentered the party, which was in full swing and, much to my surprise, running perfectly. No one cried, the witches had fun, and I even got a smile and a "good job" from the Black Widow. I should note, we never worked together again, so maybe it didn't go as well as I remembered, but hey, I'm still in business.

Years have gone by, I have thousands of events under my belt, and luckily I've only needed to pull out my Saint Cowie (patron saint of party meltdowns) medal a handful of times since my trip to Harry Potterville, when I was just a young grasshopper, hoping not to get eaten by a black widow.

# Short Acre Farm

"I'm really enjoying this, which is surprising, because you know how much I prefer dining with a rug under my feet."

This was one of the many revelations my father shared with us upon visiting the first house we owned in upstate New York.

As our catering business began to grow and prove successful, we decided that if we were going to run a husband-and-wife business out of the living room of our one-bedroom apartment in Murray Hill, we were going to need a sacred space, a house in the country where we would have one strict rule: no talk of business when we were there. A place to escape to where we were no longer business partners but simply husband and wife.

We had a very small budget for this marital sanctuary, but thankfully, soon after beginning our search, we found our dream home.

It was a twelve-hundred-square-foot farmhouse in a small hamlet outside Woodstock, New York. We called it Short Acre Farm because it sat on just under an acre of land. It had a kitchen, living room, dining room, and bathroom on the first floor and two small bedrooms on the second floor. It also had a ginormous 1970s-style hotel-sized swimming pool that was poorly maintained and a little out of place but totally perfect for us. I think the footprint of the pool was larger than the footprint of our house. We fell deeply into real estate love.

We purchased the house at a time when they were still giving out non-income-verified mortgages (which led to the demise of our economy), and we emptied our bank account to make it happen. But that was okay; we were so in love with this home, and we were going to make it ours. Every corner of the house was carefully discussed and curated; every piece of furniture we bought together had a story. We couldn't wait to run up there every weekend to plant something or paint something. It was dreamy.

About two months after we closed and I deemed it perfect for my parents to visit, I sent them an invite. Two months? Why the wait? I'll tell you. Growing up, my father always said, "There are two types of people, beach people and mountain people, and we, Mary, are beach people." Never once in my eighteen years of living under my parents' roof did we head to the mountains. Year after year, we spent all our leisure time at the beach, so you can only imagine their surprise when I told them that we bought a house in the woods.

My parents are not really outdoorsy. Nance gets her hair done twice a week. My parents have never cracked a window, ever, and they crank the AC so high in the summer that, growing up, we all wore sweaters to sleep. Our house is always so clean that you could perform surgery in any room, even the basement. I had days-of-the-week underwear and never got past Monday, since Nance did the laundry what felt like once an hour. Even the basement, usually the holding pen for memorabilia and furniture that has gone out of style, contained no trinkets of our past, as my parents hated clutter. Each year Nance would do an annual purge, which meant my sister and I would run around frantically trying to grab whatever was left of the few keepsakes Nance was gathering up to toss.

They drove up to our dream house on a cool, crisp day, which made me happy because I know how much they hate dampness. We could only afford one air conditioner at the time, so Ryan installed it in their bedroom, and we left it on with the door closed for two days until their arrival.

We toured them from the house down to the pool, at which point my father put his arms around the both of us and said, "I'm really proud of you. This is a beautiful little shack you two have here." A shack!?

The day went on, and when we got to dinner, Nance, of course, cooked the entire meal, made with half the inventory of her favorite local Italian provisions shop back home, which she brought for the two-night stay at our place.

I proudly set the table in our dining room (so impressed we had an actual dining room) with all my new plates, glassware, and linens. I wanted this dinner to be extra special. My father made one of his long, thoughtful toasts congratulating us on our beautiful, what he now called "Ricotta Shack," and we dove into a delicious meal. Halfway through dinner, he turned to my mother, looked her in the eyes, and proclaimed, "I'm really enjoying this, which is surprising, because you know how much I prefer dining with a rug under my feet."

After dinner, we sat on our back porch for about two and a half minutes until the first bug arrived, and Nance and Rob moved back inside.

I tucked them into their morgue-temperature bedroom upstairs, pointed out the new bedding (which I had even washed so it didn't have that just-out-of-the-bag smell, which my parents hate) and the nightlights on the stairwell that led them down to the one bathroom in the house, and said good night. The last thing they said was how proud they were of us and what a lovely home we had.

The next day was just as smooth, with a trip into town that caused my father to scratch his head and ponder, "How did my daughter end up in a town with so many hippies?" Kisses after breakfast the following morning, and off they went.

Ryan and I deemed the visit a huge success and laughed while we contemplated changing the custom WELCOME TO SHORT ACRE FARM sign we'd had made to WELCOME TO THE RICOTTA SHACK.

I invited them back the following month for a visit, but sadly they declined due to "previous engagements." Months went by, with invite after invite turned down with an excuse. "Your father is in a golf game." "I threw my back out." "We have to watch our neighbors' plants."

I often retraced the timeline of their visit, looking for reasons why they did not want to return but came up with nothing. The bedroom was cold, the bugs stayed outside, I got rid of the mold smell. I even supplied an array of "Poopouri" for them in the one small bathroom. Declined invitation after declined invitation, I finally mustered up the courage to ask my mother why. Why didn't they want to return to our beautiful little shack? And then finally, Nance revealed the why.

"Mary, you have to get a second bathroom. Your father spent the entire weekend peeing in a Poland Spring bottle."

# Just Eat the Doritos

One of the arduous tasks this "caterer to the stars" must endure is fulfilling celebrity riders prior to an event. To be able to demand a rider is to have made it in such a large way that you can insist on what type of flower in what color you never want to be near, what type of fancy water (it's always FIJI) must be available in abundance, and how many perfectly chilled martini glasses must be waiting in the freezer prior to your arrival.

But no matter how silly or frivolous these riders may be, I, the caterer, must meet these demands with perfect accuracy. No detail is to be missed, because if one Hostess CupCake is not offered in the preferred flavor, this could end my catering career, and the assistant who took her eye off the ball—or in this case, the cupcake—would certainly be toast. I can't tell you how many rider "inspections" I have been forced to endure.

"We specifically said eighteen pieces of farm-raised salmon. I see twenty-three," a twenty-something very hysterical assistant will hiss at me until I physically remove the five offending pieces of fish from the platter, the room, and sometimes even the building.

One thing about riders that bugs me the most is that, almost always, none of the items requested are ever actually consumed by the celebrity who supposedly requested them. I can't tell you how many bags of Cool Ranch Doritos sat sealed shut, desperately waiting for Snoop Dogg to triumphantly tear them open or how many bottles of Red Bull (the second most requested rider beverage after FIJI Water) sat unopened and dejected, not to be the object of Jay-Z's and Beyoncé's desire. When I first started out in catering, I made zero dollars a week, but if you came to my small Christopher Street studio, I always had a fridge stocked with FIJI Water and more Jo Malone scented candles than I could give away over ten Christmases. This was great for me because I was always hydrated, and my place consistently smelled like Mariah Carey's dressing room, but really, what a waste of money.

One of the most ridiculous riders I ever received stipulated that a most definitely A-list celebrity was allergic to wool, all aged cheeses, and certain types of shoe leather. Do you know how hard it is to ask all your waiters, to say nothing of every single party guest, if their shoes are made from real or fake leather? After spending the night frantically inspecting people's feet and keeping my eye out for rogue wool, the actress who was deathly allergic to everything, once she had downed two martinis, was found eating from the cheese platter with a fork and knife, donning a wool hat, and smoking cigarettes all while sitting on a *leather sofa!* Who's in the corner laughing at me, the caterer? Her assistant.

As much as I mock the rider, I hope to someday be so important that someone's only job is to make sure that my mozzarella sticks are kept both crispy and gooey and that the real Chuck Mangione can be stored in the nearest coat closet, ready to pop out and play "Feels So Good" live upon my request.

My dearest friend (who too works with high-level celebrities and loves my rider stories) and I play the "ridiculous rider game." When either of us is headed to each other's home for a simple soiree, we will send ahead our list of demands. My most recent list included the following:

- An above-ground hot tub that only plays AC/DC music
- A beige alpaca wearing a chalice cup
- A Cabbage Patch Kid from the 1980s with proper documentation
- Hot fondue in all rooms at all times
- A Corvette
- A dance floor that lights up, Michael Jackson "Beat It" style
- Oh, I almost forgot: a case of FIJI Water and a six-pack of Red Bull.

**PART III:**

# COCKTAILS

## "LOOKS LIKE
## WE MADE IT"

—Barry Manilow

# It Could Have Been Baldwin

One summer, on the very first day I began my highly antic-
ipated two-week vacation in Woodstock, I received a call
from one of our biggest and brightest celebrity clients, who
needed a last-minute party in the Hamptons. (Think big.)

In such a moment, no is just not an option. When this
client calls, you quickly turn off that Joni Mitchell record,
remove the bedsheet that you have fashioned into your
casual evening wear, jump in the shower (the one you
weren't planning on using for two weeks), and cut your
vacation short.

A few days later, I pulled into my client's driveway,
where my party captain was waiting for me with a briefing.

"Mary, I think it may be Madonna's birthday party, not
sure, but they are making quite a fuss. Did you shower?" he
asked as he looked me up and down. I showered!

While we walked up the long, beautiful driveway together, I began to think about all the amazing clients our company had been blessed to work with and, okay, for a moment allowed myself to fantasize about being a guest at one of these incredible parties rather than the girl serving the crab cakes. I could not linger in this reverie for long, however, because it was time to get to work.

The dinner began, and the waiters coming in and out of the kitchen give me updates (none food-related, of course), counting off all the A-list celebs partying in the room just outside the kitchen. None really piqued my interest until . . .

"Mary! Alec Baldwin is here."

Excuse me!? Alec!? *My* Alec!?

I *love* Alec Baldwin. I love Alec Baldwin so much that if I were him, I wouldn't let me near him. But I bet you think I am talking about the cute, young *Married to the Mob*, *Knots Landing*, or *Working Girl* Alec Baldwin. No, no, my dear friends. I love the big, messy, overweight, perfectly blown-out Alec Baldwin. My porn is a paparazzi shot of him with Jack Nicholson on a yacht in St. Barth's . . . shirt-less. Think pre–Hilaria Baldwin (Sidebar: I think Hilaria is a pretty amazing woman. Any mother of four that can do a downward dog between two garbage cans during rush hour in downtown Manhattan is tops in my book.) Point is, I *love* Alec, and he was finally within meeting distance.

Start tuning your small violin for me because this is part one of why being caterer to the stars sometimes stinks.

You know how couples mutually agree to "passes" in

their relationships, certain wildly unlikely scenarios that would give one person permission to indulge a fantasy, should it ever present itself? Couples say this knowing that they have a one in a million chance of ever finding themselves in such a lucky position: safe bet, right? Well here is the pain of my life: Ryan and I do from time to time encounter our free passes, and now mine was fewer than ten feet away. Torture!

"I need to see him up close, but I can't just walk through the party," I crazy-whispered to my captain.

So what do I do? I excuse myself from the kitchen and begin a ninja-like obstacle course through the backyard of this client's house to sneak a peek of My Alec. Fabulous landscaping, by the way. Once there, I stood outside the window, and there he was: my perfectly imperfect Alec enjoying one of my mini tuna tacos. (Take your head out of the gutter.)

I felt like Stella Dallas standing outside the window of her daughter's wedding.

And then the harsh reality of two things began to set in. One: there was a considerable piece of house standing in the way of my ever even meeting My Alec. Two: even if the universe wanted our stars to collide and I was in the exact place *The Secret* wanted me to be, I was in fact a very happily married woman.

I took one final glimpse, sighed, maybe even whispered, "We could have been something, Baldwin," and began a deflated walk back to the kitchen.

"What do you think?" my chef asked as he shoved a plate of filet in my face for the first-course approval.

"It's fine but so unfair!" I dramatically pouted as confusion spread across his face as to what fine or fair had to do with a piece of filet.

And then the kitchen door swung open, and there he was: huge, beautiful, gorgeous, My Alec in the kitchen. I looked up, and we made direct eye contact, his eyes so piercingly blue and beautiful that they actually played music, his hand outstretched to mine! The biggest hand in the entire world enveloped my small trembling one. Alec . . .

"M-M-M Mary. Nice to meet you."

"What's for dinner?" he asked, but I heard, "What are you cooking for me and then feeding me with your hands after a sweaty lovemaking session in the wine cellar?"

"Do you like Italian?" I managed to get the words out of my mouth.

"Yes, I do," he said, which I heard as, "Let's skip the sex, Giuliani. Let's go straight to marriage. You, Mary, are what I have been looking for my whole life, and I want to grow old with you."

We were quickly interrupted when the kitchen door swung open and an agent type walked in and grabbed Alec to come see someone he said was very important. And then he was gone.

In one fluid motion, I reached for my cell phone in my pocket and closed myself up inside the first private space I could find: the utility closet.

"Ryan?"

"Yes," my husband answered in a voice that said, "Why do you sound surprised that I, your husband, am answering our shared home telephone?"

"I need to tell you something. Never before has our marriage been compromised in any way... as it is right now."

Without skipping a beat, Ryan began to laugh and replied, "Is Baldwin there?"

I gulped, "Yes."

There was a knock on the door. I opened it.

My chef was there with a "get your butt back to the kitchen immediately" look. (He knew where to search for me, as I often can be found hiding in the closets of my clients' kitchens.)

"I love you, honey," I told Ryan as I hung up. Alec was back and looking for me. I walked toward him again, guided only by the blue light from his piercing eyes. Here it was . . . the moment I both dreaded and welcomed at the same time.

Sure, Ryan would be upset for a week, maybe even a month. But after we divided the assets, with him giving me the Woodstock house and me reluctantly giving him our dog, Stanley, to mend his broken heart, time would heal all wounds, and we would both realize it was for the best.

Alec stopped in front of me. He had a question.

I was ready to respond and leave my matrimonial life behind me. And then it came.

"Mary?"

"Yes, Alec?"

"Can I please have a Diet Coke? There aren't any out at the bar."

As my chef recalls, I made my way to the fridge and poured him the "saddest Diet Coke ever served."

With a simple "Thanks," he turned his back to me as he made his way out the swinging kitchen door.

"Could've Been" by the eighties pop phenomenon Tiffany began to play in the soundtrack of my mind, and with that, our romance was over.

# Mini Tuna Tacos with Italian Guacamole

While Alec may not have been interested in me, he sure was interested in these tacos.

### MAKES 24 MINI TACOS

#### TACO SHELLS

8 (6-inch) soft corn tortillas

2 tablespoons olive oil

#### TUNA

8 ounces small-diced or chopped sushi-grade tuna loin

1 tablespoon chopped Gaeta olives

1 tablespoon diced roasted peppers

1 teaspoon chopped salted capers

1 teaspoon small diced preserved lemon or lemon zest

1 tablespoon Sicilian extra virgin olive oil

Salt and pepper, to taste

#### GUACAMOLE

Juice of 1 lemon

1 clove garlic, peeled and minced

3 small or 2 medium ripe avocados

1 cup loosely packed basil leaves, chopped

¼ cup scallions, finely chopped

Salt and pepper

..........................................

Preheat the oven to 375°F.

Cut out small 2-inch circles from the larger corn tortilla. This yields 3 per tortilla.

Brush the tortilla circles with the olive oil on both sides to make them more pliable.

Place them in a mini taco shell mold, season with salt and pepper, and bake until golden brown, approximately 6 minutes. Let the shells cool and cover in an airtight container until ready to use.

Make the tuna mixture. Place tuna, olives, peppers, capers, and zest in a bowl, stir together, and season with the oil, salt, and pepper to taste. Refrigerate until ready to use.

Muddle the avocados with the garlic, basil, scallions, salt, pepper, and lemon juice to make the guacamole.

Fill the tacos with the tuna mixture and top with guacamole.

# Eating Stories

In 1985, my parents took me to see *The Goonies*, and on the car ride home, I burst into tears. When my mother asked me why I was crying, I simply responded, "Because, I think you can only take one parent to the Oscars, and I'm going to have a tough time choosing between you and Dad." (This was not the first time I mourned the high price of my inevitable success far, far in advance. Another time, after gymnastics class, across the booth from my mother at Friendly's, tears flowed again. "I sure am going to miss you when I have to leave to train for the Olympics." I could barely do a cartwheel.)

*The Goonies* had so inspired me that between the movie and the walk to the car, I was already planning the film I would make that would take me to the Academy Awards. It would be called *The Adventure Kids* (basically a *Goonies* knockoff). The next morning I got to work, calling all the kids on my block and telling them to come to my house for a "casting" of my new film. I held the auditions in my garage, where I placed a desk, a chair, my white and orange Casio keyboard, and my blue recorder. I'd play the demo song (now available on the internet for all posterity if you search for "Casio keyboard vintage 1980s demo song"), then start playing my recorder for the gang to either sing along or dance along. We all took this very seriously.

When casting was complete, I handed the lucky few copies of the rehearsal schedule, which included suggested costuming and a date for the filming. My Papa Charlie helped me fine-tune the script, and a month later *The Adventure Kids* (starring all the kids on my block: me, Lauren, Michelle, Patrick, Rachel, and Freddy) was ready to shoot. I begged my father to hire a real cameraman, he kindly obliged, and a man named Joey showed up with a camera the size of a refrigerator. I yelled "Action!" for the first time. It was roundly agreed that the shoot was a total success, and when the VHS tape arrived a month later, before even watching it, I picked up the phone, called 411, and requested and received the number for NBC. When the switchboard operator answered, I simply asked, "How do I get my film on your network?"

Even though *The Adventure Kids* did not go on to win an Oscar, my trajectory was set. I was going to be in "the business." I chased this dream for years. I tried out for all the school plays in middle school and high school, mostly getting cast in the chorus. And when I lost the battle with my parents to go to college at NYU to "hone my craft," I found all the acting and theater classes I could at Georgetown (four, to be exact) and took them all twice to fulfill a fine arts/theater minor. I even worked briefly in DuPont Circle at the Studio Theater Box Office. After college, I arrived in New York and hit the ground running, auditioning for James Lipton for a coveted spot at the Actors Studio (rejected) and standing in long lines for auditions that I learned about in *Backstage Magazine* (also rejected).

Highlights of my acting career included the following:

- I was cast as an extra in Whit Stillman's *The Last Days of Disco*, during which I would spend a week dancing in a cold warehouse in New Jersey to no music with a bunch of other extras.

- I was cast as an extra in an NBC movie of the week about Sammy "The Bull" Gravano. I wore a tight leather dress and walked up and down the same street for six hours.

- And finally, my big break, one line in an off-off-Broadway production of Eric Bogosian's *Suburbia* at the Triad Theater, playing a Pakistani terrorist who pulls a gun on some kids trying to steal from the 7-Eleven. My one line was in Urdu.

This dream of mine was going nowhere, and as I got

older, I was unable to will my destiny into being as I had when I was younger, with Cameraman Joey at my disposal. So I shelved my dream and resolved to throw myself into my new role as caterer. Until one day, the itch came back.

The idea came to me in the middle of the night, which is always the time that big ideas come to me. I had seen Nora Ephron's *Love, Loss, and What I Wore* the night before with my friend Lee. That show was all I had been thinking about. I was obsessed with the simplicity of it. A piece of clothing leads to a story. Ding, ding, ding! I was going to get back on the stage. I could combine my successful catering career with my not-so-successful acting career and give it one last try. I was going to write a one-woman show titled *If You Can't Join 'Em, Serve 'Em*. I would share my stories in front of a sold-out audience while waiters delivered mini bites of food or small sips of drinks on cue, right to the seats, to coincide with the plot line. This was sure to win me a Tony or whatever the equivalent is for dinner theater. A Bologne?

The first story I wrote was titled "Can the Waiters Come Dressed as Pilgrims?" about a difficult client and a Thanksgiving gone terribly wrong. The food was turkey and cranberry on mini pumpkin muffins. Perfect! The next story, "Guess Who's Not Coming to Dinner," was all about my dream dinner party guest list. I was so excited. So excited, in fact, that I convinced my business partners that I needed a small leave from my catering business to move to Woodstock full-time to write this play. Thank you, Michele, Ryan, and

Ryan for encouraging this, which would end up being one of many walkabouts I've taken from my business to chase a dream.

Once I had organized a bunch of stories, I realized I had never written a play before, and when my attempt to use the RoughDraft software backfired, it was time to call in the big guns. Enter Jo Adler, a friend from Georgetown: she was a freshman when I was a senior, and she was one of those old souls, wise beyond her years, beautiful, talented, whip-smart, and funny. She was also my only friend who moved to California to work in "the business." Of course, she had quick success, producing a few blockbuster movies and a documentary.

I sent Jo my stories, and like magic, she was *in*. I convinced her to move to Woodstock for the month of August to write alongside me. It all sounded so romantic. Two friends, in a rustic farm cottage, in one of the most fabled artists' colonies on the planet, writing a script. Mary and Jo were going to be the next Matt and Ben.

We took walks with a small tape recorder to capture my stories; we went to Target and bought Post-its, notebooks, and dry-erase boards. We wrote during the day and at night saw bands perform at the small-town dive-y bars, surrounding ourselves with other kinds of artists, all of us slaves to the muse.

When the script was finished, we planned a sneak-peek performance at my parents' house in Montauk. It was the summer, and because of my newly achieved "caterer to the stars" status, *Hamptons Magazine* even agreed to cover the performance. Finally! This was it! It had taken me years of dreaming to get to this point. I was going to make it. I was finally going to be a star!

How did it go?

An utter disaster. When the mic turned on and I looked out into the audience, I had crippling stage fright. I forgot my lines and yelled "Line!" so many times to Jo during the performance that it became comical. I knew my performance wasn't great by the look on my parents' faces, which started as pride and quickly turned to mortification. And while the food cues were perfect and the food couldn't have been more beautiful or creative, I was a dud. When it was over, people said things to me like, "There's no place to go from here but up" and "First time is always the hardest." I was not the actress I had thought I was for all those years.

After the show, I was broken. Sad, depressed, devastated. I had no talent. I had spent years chasing this dream, and now it was finally over. I was just going to be a caterer—that's all, that's it. I took the week off from work to recover mentally and physically and lay on my couch in my pajamas. Until I got a call from my dad. "Mary, listen to this!"

He then went on to read the following letter from *The East Hampton Star* about me. And it was a rave!

# THE  STAR

Grandest Stage
Montauk
June 19, 2010

Dear Editor,

The grandest stage on Earth on Saturday evening last was
set along the Old Montauk Highway on a bluff 60 feet
above the Atlantic Ocean, where the eastern horizons
slowly turned peacock indigo behind a set of white drapes
that hung on poles near the edge to suggest theatrical
fantasy. The wide, ivory beaches unreeled below, and the
gentle surf fell melodiously on the sands. Weathered old
pines silhouetted themselves against the sky to add a
Buddhist flavor to it all. The light breezes were cool and
perfumed with roses and honeysuckle.

Not to be upstaged by this grand stage was the biggest
problem of the evening. Mary Giuliani solved it in an
instant. All she had to do was smile.

In the warm pink and gold spotlight of late afternoon
sunshine, Mary glowed. She is an actress who blames her
parents and many friends for giving her an overblown
sense of self-esteem. With her husband, Ryan, she was

host at their house for friends, neighbors and loved ones. It was the seaside debut of *If You Can't Join 'Em, Serve 'Em*, which Mary wrote with her friend Joanna Adler and produced by Ryan Giuliani. It was Mary's first theater presentation before an invited audience.

Barbara Koppel, the brilliant documentary filmmaker, and Michael Lang, the Puckish mind behind the actual Woodstock festival, sat happily together to cheer Mary on. There were two dozen more family, friends, and admirers seated at small tables on the lawn in front of the great stage and the sea and sky. Mary is a fit and beautiful woman dressed simply and perfectly in a tailored silk skirt and blouse. She has long chestnut hair and a twinkle of big-time Italian mischief in her brown eyes.

When her butterflies fluttered away, Mary Giuliani told true stories about her family, which has lived in Montauk for seventy-two years. She thanked her grandmother Lucille who came in 1938 to a Hither Hills dune overlooking the sea, spread her arms to God and said, "This is where we will be."

So she built the first inn along the Old Montauk Highway in Montauk, the Wavecrest, and the family prospered.

As Mary told her humorous stories about how she became the caterer to those who can pay for the very best, a crew of ballet-like waiters circulated about the tables on cue with artfully prepared and plated dainty morsels that cleverly fit in with Mary's stories and even moved the plot along.

Mary's catering side produced a potent purple potion in elegant Thomas Jefferson crystal glasses in honor of a very funny story about catering for Oprah Winfrey. Along came a nugget of steamed lobster in a tiny crust, to be washed down with a small pony of golden beer. Then came authentic little pigs in blankets. Then a white chocolate "s'more" the size of a quarter, and finally a small, witty V-glass of vanilla milkshake with a small square of crusty, chewy brownie perched on the lips of the glass. If the word *chic* means anything any longer, that drink is chic.

By the time Mary's act was over, she was the most huggable person on the grandest stage on Earth, and the entire audience had become part of her fabled Montauk family.

When *Serve 'Em* gets to Off Broadway, where it is headed, the stage will shrink in grandeur but Mary and her stories are sure to grow.

—Barnard Collier

I cried tears of gratitude. I was back!

And while *If You Can't Join 'Em, Serve 'Em* never did make it to a proper stage, years later, the bug was back and I morphed the idea into an event titled *Eating Stories*. I asked pals to join me this time and share their stories, *Moth*-like, at the 2015 NYC Wine & Food Festival. The sold-out event was such a success that *New York Magazine* asked us to put on *Eating Stories* at Vulture Festival in 2017. I'm working on another version for the future. It's a formula that people seem to love: storytelling with the food that makes the narrative come alive. And something else happened along the way: I realized I had made it to the stage. No disco moves without the music, no Urdu, just me serving up stories, Mary-style. I'd like to think Nora would approve.

# Lists

Some people make lists to keep them organized. Not me. My lists serve no real purpose other than as a place to catalogue my most delusional dreams.

## Things I'd Love to Do with Oprah

In my first book, *The Cocktail Party*, which can be found wherever books are sold, shelved under "This book would have done a lot better if she were part of the *Housewives* franchise," I shared a story about a party I catered during which I waited patiently for Oprah to arrive. I fantasized about her falling in love with me upon taking one bite of my mini short rib truffle grilled cheese and whisking me off to Oprahland, where we would, wrapped in Spanx, delight in each other's company by the fire. That never happened.

But if it had, I'd be prepared with material for instant best friendship with the following:

1. Take a tandem bike ride

2. Write and perform a song for her on my recorder

3. Master one dance routine that will be "ours" and perform it as "our thing" at parties and special events

4. Get perms and then laugh at how bad we both look with perms

5. Eat a funny brownie and try to pronounce "Tchoupitoulas" (a street in New Orleans)

6. TP someone's lawn and then feel so guilty about it the next day that we buy them a new house

7. Go to IKEA on a Saturday and hang out in one of the sample living rooms all day; eat meatballs with lingonberry sauce for lunch; push each other through the store in the wheelie carts

8. Reenact the scene from *The Notebook* when Rachel McAdams (played by me) yells at Ryan Gosling (played by Oprah) for not writing, and he yells back, "I wrote you 365 letters. I wrote you every day for a year! I wrote you every day!"

9. Make her knock on random people's doors and observe their reaction when she asks them if she can sleep over or use the bathroom

10. Eat cheese

## Ladies' Luncheon Guest List (Dead or Alive)

I'm not so much a lady who lunches, but I am someone who fantasizes often about whom I would lunch with (dead or alive) if I were. I dream of one round table (I love round tables) and the place settings would feature only the following: a martini glass and individual shaker and colorful mismatched plates. There would be no flowers in the center of the table, just petit four stands and cake plates of varying heights filled to the brim with pigs in a blanket.

1. Lucille Ball

2. Lily Tomlin

3. Gilda Radner

4. Penny Marshall

5. Nora Ephron

6. Billie Holiday

7. Nell Carter

8. Dorothy Parker

9. Lady Gaga

10. Betty White (I read she attributes her longevity to copious amounts of vodka and hot dogs)

## Men I'd Love to Dance With (Dead or Alive)

I love to dance. One of my favorite pre-entertaining rituals is to remove my shoes, blast music (I am currently really enjoying the Bread, Hall & Oates, and Sinatra Pandora stations), and start cooking or setting the table for the party. Nothing says party success more than impromptu dancing erupting at one of your soirees. My grandmother used to say to men she admired, "I'd love to kick off my shoes and dance with you." Well, here's my list.

1. Michael Jackson

2. Jesus

3. Jackson Browne

4. Mickey Dolenz

5. Jackie Gleason

6. Sherman Hemsley (George Jefferson on *All in the Family*)

7. Pauly D from *Jersey Shore*

8. Fred Berry (Rerun from *What's Happening!!*)

9. John Belushi

10. Jacque Pépin

# My Date with the Barefoot Contessa

As I'm sure you've realized by now, I have an extremely active imagination. I've imagined myself in every possible scenario involving meeting someone I admire. It's usually some fantastical scene that goes like this: I meet this person, and they finally see in me what I've always seen in myself—greatness with a touch of something so unique and remarkable that they want to whisk me away, make me their best friend, tell me their secrets, invite me to their mahjong game. Note: since I admire a lot of older Jewish women, odds of them playing mahjong? Pretty high.

If you start your career at twenty-five, it's a lot like getting married young. You're bonded to something for better for worse, and even if your tastes, dreams, and desires change, you still have to live with all of it—the terrible plates you loved when you made your wedding registry and that same joke you've heard your spouse tell hundreds of times but never found funny. (Ryan, you know I'm talking about the Bingo in Japan story. They only laugh to be polite.)

Well, by the time I hit thirty-five, I had reached a true lull in my career. The mini grilled cheese that I co-opted and declared "life changing" were now just little sandwiches. For six years, I ate, prayed, and loved every minute of the late nights, frantic clients, crazy hours, and bleeding feet that my catering company gave me in spades. But at thirty-five, I started to ask myself, "What's next? What if this is it?" I was struggling to start a family and was shifting focus to what I assumed would be a new chapter in my life, so I spent a lot of time on this. I mean a lot. And I started to get resentful. When I wasn't working, I was crying and lamenting that all I had was this catering company, while all my other friends now had actual tiny little lives demanding their care and attention. That's when I started to take my work for granted and, okay, I'll say it: I was bitter.

Well, I finally did get pregnant after years of trying. I was pregnant for all of eighteen days. Then, while on my way out to Montauk to do a party for one of my favorite clients, I began to miscarry in the parking lot of the IGA supermarket. With no time to dwell or cry, I had to get to my clients' house to do what I did best: work.

Disconnected and sad, although grateful for the distraction and knowing that when I was finally alone, I'd be a complete mess, I started to tray up some hors d'oeuvres. I chatted with my client, who always enjoyed an escape into his kitchen during a party, as much as he is a great host. My client happened to be the CEO of a very large and popular fashion chain, and as we chatted away, I was tempted to ask, "Do I at least get a lifetime discount on cashmere sweaters for completing my miscarriage in your kitchen today?"

Most of the day, I stayed in the kitchen and stared out sadly into the party, wondering if I was destined to watch other people live their happy lives while I'd die alone with my crab cakes.

But shortly into my lament, my gaze was interrupted by what I can only call a divine vision. Really, could it be!? Is that Ina? Is that Ina Garten? Is that Jeffrey!? Holy grilled cheese, it was!

"Mary, I would like you to meet someone," my favorite client announced as he entered the kitchen. There she was, Ina, the Barefoot Contessa. And Jeffrey!

Suddenly I forgot my tears and my pain and moved right into blubbering, brain-disconnected-from-mouth fool. I smiled and spoke sentences that made no sense, and through the power of delusion, I remember Ina was very kind and sincere and seemed genuinely interested in what I had to say. She asked me (*me!*) for my business card and introduced me to Jeffrey! She complimented me on my mini grilled cheeses and whimsical serving trays and left the kitchen with a warm goodbye.

Well, suffice it to say that the day took a turn for the better, and while still heartbroken that it was not my time to become a mother, I took my Ina meeting as a sign to put my head back into my business. I had created something pretty terrific—in fact, great enough for the Barefoot Contessa to notice me.

The Monday after that party, it was like starting fresh at work. I wrote a new hors d'oeuvre list, began to dream up even more creative serving trays, and recommitted myself to my business, all in the name of Ina.

A few weeks passed (try to stay with me because this gets good).

Hurricane Irene hit the Hudson Valley, my home away from home in New York. My fellow neighbors were unprepared, shocked, and devastated, and lives were turned upside down. There was nothing to do but start digging out, so Ryan and I drove into Phoenicia (the town neighboring Woodstock) and asked where we should go and what we should do.

Helping with the cleanup was just what the doctor ordered. We were handed two shovels and told to start down a road, find any house that needed help, and get to work. That was it. It felt great to actually do something. There were about twelve homes on the street where we were standing, so we picked up our shovels and headed in.

We walked into the backyard of a home that was badly damaged; the water had come up to the second floor of the house. The patio furniture was lodged under the deck that surrounded the pool, and the pool itself was brown with clay and dirt. There were about seven of us. I was given gloves, paper towels, and a bucket of warm water. Ryan and one of two men started to lug the large furniture to the backyard for us to hose down and try to save.

We cleaned off diplomas, pictures, books, remote controls, anything we could find: all in the name of saving memories for this household of strangers.

In the rubble, I found a small green tin box (retro-green, my favorite kind). It was a recipe box. I am a sucker for an old-fashioned recipe box, especially one with handwritten cards (you know the kind: with that beautiful script of grandmothers). I grabbed this box and took it to the owner of the house, offering it up with joy and saying, "I think we can save this if we put it in the sunlight and let it dry." A huge smile came over the face of this exhausted but grateful woman who had lost almost everything. She practically embraced the box, telling me that the cards had belonged to her mother, and she had always planned to pass them on to her daughter, who worked in food television. It was obvious that this soggy heirloom meant the world to her.

"Well then this *must* be saved," I enthusiastically agreed.

A week later, I received a call from a producer from Ina's show who told me that Ina had enjoyed our meeting in my client's kitchen. Ina wanted me to come on the show and cook with her. Me!? I couldn't say yes fast enough.

Ryan drove us from my parents' home in Montauk to Ina's house in East Hampton. It was raining heavily, and I felt like I was having a mini-stroke in anticipation. The sight of a beautiful and sweet woman about my age, who greeted me at the door, was calming. I was *so* nervous. She invited me to sit and hang out for a moment until we walked onto the set.

I think this incredibly kind producer could see how nervous I was, and she carried on our conversation instead of going back to her emails or the obviously endless list of important things she needed to do. Then this happened.

"Do you live out here?"

"No, I live in New York, but my heart is in Woodstock, where my husband and I have a home." She told me her mother lived in Phoenicia. "Oh wow! How did she do in the storm?" I asked.

"Not well. Her home was destroyed; they had water up to the second floor," the producer said.

Water, flood, second floor, daughter works in food television, retro-green recipe box, wet handwritten cards: it all popped into my head at once. Goosebumps ran up and down my entire body. Time stopped for a second. With wide eyes, I said, "I think I may have met your mom!"

I started to tell her the story, and we realized that it *was* her mother's backyard where I found the recipe box, and here we were, connected in the Barefoot Contessa's kitchen.

The day went on. Ina was as warm and impressive as you would imagine. Whatever draws you to watch her show, multiply that by a thousand, and that is what the day was like. She soothed my shaking hands by offering me lavender lotion from her kitchen drawer while I was struggling to make grilled cheese, but more importantly she inspired me to continue doing what I love. She showed me that my business could be one of the great loves of my life.

The baby, the no-baby, the hurricane, the producer's grandmother's recipe box, the devastation, the repair. The beauty and the pain of all these connections.

When we wrapped the show, I went to find the producer—the woman who not only calmed my anxious spirit but connected the dots between my worlds—and lo and behold, she had something to show me. She had emailed her mom while I was shooting with Ina, and her mom sent her a picture of me, covered in mud, holding her grandmother's recipe box.

And as my pal Ina would say, "How great is *that*!?"

# Mini Grilled Cheeses with Pepper Jack, Mango, and Watercress

### MAKES 24 PIECES

**6 slices soft white bread**

**6 teaspoons unsalted butter, melted**

**6 tablespoons mango puree (from store-bought concentrate, simmered until reduced and thick)**

**6 tablespoons chopped watercress**

**6 slices pepper jack cheese**

Brush both sides of each slice of bread with butter and mango puree.

Arrange the watercress over the top of one slice of bread, place the cheese on top of the watercress, and top with the second slice of bread.

Heat a griddle on medium-high. Grill the sandwich for approximately 1 minute on each side, or until bread is golden brown and cheese is melted.

Remove from pan and set sandwich aside to cool.

Once cooled, cut into 8 small triangles. Pieces can be served at room temperature or stored and reheated in the oven at 350°F for 10 minutes.

# Mini Grilled Cheeses with Spicy Buffalo Chicken, Pepper Jack, and Blue Cheese

MAKES 24 PIECES

6 slices soft white bread

12 teaspoons unsalted butter, melted

6 tablespoons blue cheese at room temperature, crumbled

½ cup heavy cream

½ cup shredded chicken breast

4 tablespoons hot sauce

6 slices pepper jack cheese

Brush both sides of each slice of bread with the butter.

Place the blue cheese and heavy cream in a food processor fitted with a steel blade and process until smooth. Spread the pureed blue cheese over the top of one side of each slice of bread.

In a small bowl, mix together the chicken and hot sauce and arrange it over the blue cheese puree on one slice of bread. Place the pepper jack cheese on top of the chicken and cover it with the other slice of bread, blue cheese puree-side down.

Heat a griddle on top of the stove on medium-high. Grill for about 2 to 3 minutes on each side, or until the bread is golden brown and the cheese is melted. Slice the sandwich into 8 small pieces.

# Waiting for Godot
# Woodstock-Style

"When do you think she'll let us go home? I'm really tired."

. The first and only time I heard these words whispered at one of my events, they came from the lips of a famous heavy metal rock star who is notorious for late nights and wild parties. This was a true indication that things were not going well.

Earlier in the week, I had arrived at our home in Woodstock and received a voicemail that launched me into orbit in the best possible way. It was a short message—"You rang, Miss?"—with no call-back number. Puzzled, since he was the one who had called me, I had to listen at least twenty times in a row until I finally realized who it was, and then I listened to it some more. I don't want to blow anyone's cover, but it was from a very iconic, notoriously mysterious actor whose biggest blockbuster movies rhyme with "Shaddycack" and "Boastgusters."

The reason for the magical voicemail? The aforementioned comedic genius was in town, shooting a film, and a mutual friend thought we would "hit it off as pals," so she passed along my number. Since he is notoriously unreachable, I gave our mutual pal my schedule for the week to share with his "people," should he feel inclined to stop by for pancakes and fireworks, an afternoon dance party, or midnight nachos, all things that happen on a typical weekend at our house in Woodstock. The waiting for (let's call him) Mill Burray began in earnest.

Of course, my friend couldn't confirm his attendance at any of the above, but she passed the itinerary along to him, including my idea that I also could drive behind his golf cart with a full wet bar if he took to the local Woodstock links, available to shake him up a quick Negroni between holes.

As the week came and went, I sent short texts to our mutual friend, announcing my whereabouts—things like, "Bingo at The Pines!" or "Karaoke at The Lodge!" or "Swimming at Big Deep!"—thinking that Mill Burray would enjoy all these activities and might happily materialize, but the week went on with no enchanted meeting. I sent one final message saying, "In case he'd prefer a more private hang, I'm having a little party at my barn on Saturday night and it will be laid back and low key. Just some close friends." I hit "send" with more than a note of bittersweet; since his film would be wrapping shortly, and this was my last night in Woodstock for a month, this would seemingly be our last chance for an encounter.

When our pal responded, "Great. Here's what he likes to drink, just in case," I took this as a definite sign that he *would* be coming and announced to *everyone* I had invited, after deeming them Mill Burray worthy, "*Guess who's coming?!?!?!*" the second they showed up at the party.

The problem with waiting for a surprise guest who's not really a surprise, once you've put all your guests on high alert, is that not only are you excited every time headlights illuminate the driveway, but all your guests are on pins and needles, too. So when a friend enters your party and is *not* Mill Burray, he or she is met with a terribly disappointed "Oh, just you" look from the whole crowd rather than a warm welcome. Epic party foul. Even when the hot dog delivery guy arrived with dawgs and all the fixings (from my favorite local hot dog vendor, Dallas Hot Wieners), instead of getting my usual open-armed hello and happy wiener smile, he too was met with the "Oh, just you" face.

Hours went by, as disappointment followed disappointment. I even ran to the house to grab a chocolate cake, which I had made the previous night from my mother's recipe, in an attempt to liven up the party, but nothing worked. Guests were now growing tired, antsy, and disappointed, and when I heard my rock star pal ask another friend if I was *ever* going to let them leave, I realized I was giving off a terrorist vibe instead of a happy hostess vibe, literally holding my guests hostage at my party. Around 1 a.m. I decided that our guest would not be showing and called it. Let me tell you, it was equivalent to yelling, "Fire!! Fire!!" the way they all hastily kissed me goodnight and fled from the barn.

Totally bummed out yet still hungry since I had not eaten, I sliced off a piece of chocolate cake, cranked up Elvis Costello's "Peace, Love and Understanding," and danced around barefoot, dropping crumbs everywhere, still holding on to some sort of hope that Mill would barge into the barn and join me. When the song was over, I blew out the candles, closed the doors of the barn, and walked home to my house, listening to the voicemail a few more times before falling asleep.

# My Mom's Friend Rita's Chocolate Cake

This recipe was given to my mother by her good friend Rita in the 1970s. It's a really quick, really easy, no-skill-required, half-box-mix, half-homemade cake that leaves your crowd happy. It even makes you feel like you have some baking skills.

### MAKES ONE 8-INCH CAKE

1 (16.5-ounce) box dark chocolate fudge cake mix

4 eggs

½ cup vegetable oil (they used Wesson back then, but melted coconut oil would be great, too)

1 (3.9-ounce) package instant chocolate pudding

1 (12-ounce) package semisweet chocolate chips

1 (8-ounce) container sour cream

Preheat oven to 350°F. Grease an 8-inch cake pan.

Mix all the above ingredients together, adding in the chocolate chips last.

Pour in cake pan and bake for 25 to 30 minutes.

Serve to a disappointed crowd.

# Longing to Create

I've turned my back on New York City not once but twice.

The first year of our marriage, after living in the city for three years, Ryan and I took a day trip to Brooklyn (Carroll Gardens, to be specific) from our West Village apartment and on the spot rented the floor-through of a brownstone. We had been accosted by a small Italian lady who lured us to her house with the promise of a homemade meatball and an apartment with not one but two bathrooms. We lived in Carroll Gardens for exactly six months, above her very Italian family, including her husband, Santo, who judged me daily for working and not staying home to cook and clean for my husband. He failed to catch on that my husband was actually "in between jobs" during the time we lived there and that I was the one taking the F train into the city to pay the rent.

When 9/11 hit, I used my sadness to say out loud to

Ryan what I had been dying to admit, that I had made a mistake, that I hated living in Brooklyn and desperately wanted to move back to Manhattan. I swore when we finally moved back (after a short detour living in my parents' basement) that I'd never leave again.

Well, friends, never say never, because seven years later, a few years after we opened Mary Giuliani Catering & Events, it happened again. I happened upon this quote by Anaïs Nin that perfectly describes how I was feeling: "I'm restless. Things are calling me away. My hair is being pulled by the stars again." Yes, restless again, hair pointing directly north. Ryan and I found ourselves frequently escaping the city and heading north to a small town called Piermont, which boasted a romantic Sausalito feel and such shiny artistic residents as Bill Murray, Al Pacino, Lorraine Bracco, and Mikhail Baryshnikov. Every time on the way in and out of the town, we would pass a huge red-brick loft building that sat smack in the middle of the small riverside town with pastel painted Victorian homes, and we would slow down the car, look out, and ask each other, "Who lives there?"

One day, a FOR RENT sign was hanging outside our huge red-brick loft building. I begged Ryan to pull over. He fought me, as I think he knew that once I saw the inside, there would be no turning back. And he was right. I almost passed out when we entered the ginormous five-thousand-square-foot loft with thirty-five-foot ceilings, original windows, crown moldings, two large fireplaces, and so much light you needed sunglasses to look around.

"I *have* to live there. I have several articles where I am described as 'caterer to the stars.' This space was built for her . . . I mean, me." I built my argument strongly to Ryan, who, by the time we made it back over the George Washington Bridge into Manhattan, had broken and allowed me to call the landlord and tell her we'd take it. A month later, we moved in.

Our business was really taking off. I was starting to get some nice press. We had the most money in the bank we'd ever had, and I found myself relaxing easily into the "looks like we made it" phase of my life. This loft was my way of saying, "Look how well we're doing!" which, for anyone who knows me, is not typical Mary behavior.

But it wasn't a typical year. The loft was so huge, we played tennis indoors in our underwear, and when we realized we had moved just a tad too far for our friends to easily visit, we sent buses to pick them up in the city for parties that lasted two whole days. The parties were incredible, next-level really, equipped with crazy eclectic guests, Europeans who didn't ask permission to smoke indoors, celebrities. One time a woman showed up dressed in a Cher costume and danced with another woman who was topless, save for the henna she had painted on her boobs. I served huge platters of paella from oversized pans, and when the bar was empty, we pulled wine from the cases and started drinking straight from the bottles. Our friends from the city had no idea where they were going when they got on the bus and still absentmindedly ask from time to time, "Do you remember that crazy loft where we used to party?" as though it had been a dream.

Above the huge loft was a small glass room that you could only access by climbing up a twenty-foot ladder. If you wanted to bring anything up there with you, your supplies came up and down in a metal bucket attached to a string. I quickly claimed the tower as mine and turned this small glass studio into my art and writing room. Never having even picked up a paint brush before, I sent up in the bucket some paper, canvases, paints, a CD player, a few CDs (Kenny Rogers, the Beatles' *Love* soundtrack and *White Album*, Carly Simon, and the Blues Traveler's *Travelers and Thieves* album.) I would go up there for hours, sometimes with a bottle of wine, sometimes two, and ponder my desire to be an artist. I'd send silly notes or pictures I painted down the bucket to Ryan and ask in return that he send back up another bottle of wine.

No real art was ever created up there; mostly, I spent my time in that little glass room longing. I longed for the one thing we could not create: a child. I realized that as much as I told everyone I was okay that Ryan and I could not make a baby, I was slowly unraveling. The lie was catching up with me. I was longing so deeply that nothing I created or drank or smoked up in that studio filled the hole.

It was in this loft in Piermont that I first realized that Ryan and I had been married for ten years and had no prospect of a child on the horizon. I accepted that I would never be a mother, or at least birth my own child. In that small glass room, I quietly, alone, mourned my fertility, and while all our friends were having children, we were struggling with what it meant to be a childless married couple of ten years. So we attempted to create a new normal.

Our year of escape in our gigantic loft in Piermont included many games of underwear tennis, drinking in bars with strangers, and then, when the bar closed, inviting them over to dance. These new friends did not ask where our kids were or why we didn't have any. Our friends with kids stopped coming over, or we stopped inviting them. Family visits were sparse. We now preferred single, unattached, older, artistic guests. I began taking stock of how many famous friends we now had, like I was amassing my very own star collection.

When we traveled, which we did a lot that year, we'd assume aliases, Buck and Layla, and end up with strangers in our hotel rooms until all hours of the night, one time with a few cast members from *Gossip Girl*. One time we were invited to fly home on a private plane by someone we met the night before.

When back in Piermont, we tried to convince each other that this loft was our new life: crazy parties, hedonism, no rules, hiding in rooms that needed ladders. I was angry. I had done everything right, or so I thought. If God didn't want me to be a mom, then I was going to be wild.

One night during a party at the loft, we and some of our new friends, whom we had known for all of a week, had a few too many bottles of wine and decided at midnight to take a limo into the city to an exclusive nightclub that had no sign on the front door to dance until the sun came up. We blasted music so loud the driver rolled up the divider, and we laughed the whole way into the city about how our friends with kids could never do this anymore. How lucky we were! I found myself not caring at all that one of the girls was sitting a little too close to Ryan and made no effort to lower my skirt when I saw her boyfriend's eyes fixed on how short it was. Things were becoming more and more blurry.

The car ride home was even wilder, and when it was over, I had never felt worse in my entire life. It was an empty bucket kind of sadness and loneliness, dark and terrifying. When I asked the driver to pull over, I realized, hunched over on the side of the Palisades Parkway, that it wasn't the vodka that had made me sick. It was this life we were trying to escape into, which wasn't ours and would never be ours.

The next day, in my glass room, with a rocket hangover in session, I painted another something terrible and then scribbled a note to Ryan, folded it, and placed it into the metal bucket. It read:

I'm scared of how lost we are in all this space. I'm scared this space is too big for us at a time when we need to be close. I want to be near you, not above you in a tower or across a living room the size of a tennis court. I don't want to share you. I think we should move back to the city, to a smaller space. I don't want space or chaos. I want you. I miss our friends, I miss our family.

PS: Please write me back and please send up another bottle of wine and a slice of pizza or some Tums.

A month later, we moved back to Chelsea, to an eight-hundred-square-foot apartment on 17th Street and 10th Avenue, and with all that space gone, I was ready to create.

## Bitters and Soda, My #1 Hangover Cure

Of all the remedies I've tried, nothing works better than a simple glass of bitters and soda. It also goes perfectly with a bacon, egg, and cheese sandwich if you need a little extra help. I love Angostura bitters, which have a great history. The company was started by a doctor who produced medical tinctures to alleviate stomach ailments. There are lots of fancy and flavorful bitters available today, but Angostura remains my favorite.

MAKES 1 DRINK

........................

Club soda

Bitters

Fresh fruit wedges (optional)

........................................................

Pour one glass of club soda on ice. Add 5 to 6 dashes of bitters.

You can also add fresh fruit wedges. This will make you feel like you're doing something healthy.

# Games People Play

I come from a long line of party throwers, my grandmother Lucille being one of the best. As the owner of several hotels in Montauk, she was required to entertain thousands of tourists each summer. She threw Hawaiian-themed luaus and movie nights on the beach; she even had her own cocktail lounge, which she named The Sea Witch. But the gold standard of all invites at that time was one to her Saturday night dinner parties.

What made this party so special was the carefully curated and highly eclectic guest list. It was not uncommon for a local fisherman to be seated next to a senator or a young Hollywood starlet to be seated with Lucille's dry cleaner. She loved forcing people who wouldn't normally even say hello not only to acknowledge each other but to truly interact, seated next to each other during her whimsical dinners, playing one of her many party games.

I was too young to ever attend these parties as a guest, but she did let me help her set the table from time to time. She would use her finest crystal and china and linens from her travels around Europe, and then she would send me to her supply closet, out of which she'd instruct me to grab a dirty old brown paper bag filled with five-cent gag toys, like kazoos, Groucho Marx glasses, fake chatter teeth, and, my personal favorite, a windup monkey who dropped his pants to reveal his little monkey boner.

I always thought the word *boner* was hilarious, second to *hand job*.

It was my job to tape these gifts under each guest's chair, and then later in the night, if my grandmother sensed a lull in party energy, or the dinner conversation took a sharp political turn, or she simply just wanted to redirect focus to one conversation instead of many, she would clink her glass and announce, "Please reach under your seat to find your surprise." What a hoot it was to see grown adults blowing up whoopee cushions. A wonderful icebreaker (an entertaining term that became popular in the 1960s).

A few years ago, I became a member of a dinner club that never had fewer than eight or more than ten guests (which, by the way, is the perfect size for a dinner party).

At these parties, as was the case with my grandmother's soirees, the guests were always different and consisted of a perfectly curated mix of common folk, A-list celebs, rock stars, writers, chefs, athletes, producers, and directors. Just like Lucille's. You would receive this coveted invite a week prior, and it was always a solo invite—if you got lucky, you could bring a friend or, even better, your spouse if he or she made the cut. You never asked who else would be there; you either accepted or declined and were always pleasantly surprised to see with whom you would be sharing the table.

No matter whose table I'm sharing (and because of heredity and too many glasses of wine) when I sense the table becoming disconnected or when conversation hit a lull, I say, "Okay, let's go around the table. Name the first concert you attended and the name of the person who gave you your first hand job." Oh, Lucille, I guess the apple doesn't fall far.

The Elton John (Yellow Brick Road Tour) answer always impressed, as did anyone who saw Led Zeppelin, The Doors, or Hendrix live. Dead shows were always followed with the exact location, either city or venue, and what happened in the parking lot prior to the show. Bowie showed you were sophisticated. Barry Manilow always made the table laugh, and the Jackson's Victory Tour most likely meant you were the son or daughter of a celebrity because, as anyone who grew up in the 1980s knows, that was one of *the* hardest concert tickets to come by.

The hand job stories were blurted out, with first and last names and specific locations, very quickly, like in a social Tourette's kind of way. "Dave Marcus, tennis camp, summer of freshman year!" almost as if they were reciting a ball-game statistic. Some people would take passes, some didn't remember, some delighted in sharing the memory of both giving and receiving on the same night, and one time a very famous rock star took the tone of the party game way down to his preferred setting (morose) by looking at us all coldly (with a certain "Fuck you, Caterer Girl") and awkwardly, deliberately, responding, "My babysitter." Silence followed as everyone took huge swills from their wine goblets. Game over.

Given how much the world has changed and the rate at which sexuality continues to morph and toggle, I wonder now if we can still play games like these without offending. To me, a windup monkey with an erection and saying "hand job" to a table full of strangers still count as good clean fun. And also? The word *boner* is funny in every generation.

# Maeby Gala

In the sixth grade, I got my period. Naturally, this happened on the same day I decided to

(a) wear white pants to school, and

(b) perform my newly choreographed freeform dance number in the cafeteria that I titled "The Baryshnikov," and

(c) end the dance number with a grand finale, during which I jumped up on a lunchroom table, kicked up my feet, and assumed a wide-legged stance, arms in the air à la "Hallelujah!"

No applause this time? This number had slayed the lunchroom crowd in previous incarnations. My previously adoring fans looked at me with disgust—well, more like horror. Like they were witnessing a grisly murder scene. My white pants were white no more.

"Do I have to go to school?" I asked my mom, begging her with a combination of wretched, vomit-inducing cramps and embarrassment. Thankfully my mom let me not only stay home from school but also watch TV all day. But there was not enough *Price Is Right*, *Press Your Luck*, or *Days of Our Lives* to make me feel better—physically or emotionally. Something was wrong.

I didn't snap out of my depression until my best friend, who also happened to be the coolest, best-looking boy in school (I think he took pity on me), called me to say, "It wasn't that bad. It was actually kinda funny." He remains one of my favorite people to this day. I love you, Derek Silberstein.

And while I was able to get over what I came to call the Baryshnikov Massacre, this sadly wasn't the pinnacle of reproductive madness for young Mary. I suffered month after month from my period. During high school, it was days home from school; during college, it was missed classes; and in my professional life, it was missed meetings, plans with friends, nights out for fun, and then the ultimate miss: motherhood. At twenty-seven, after a four-hour surgery (during the big New York City blackout) to remove two cysts the size of tennis balls from my right and left ovaries, I was told it would be incredibly difficult, if not impossible, for me to conceive a child. Impossible? I didn't "do" impossible.

After I had been married for two years, I heard someone use the word *endometriosis* for the first time in the fourteen years (including three emergency room visits) of suffering from my period. What is endometriosis?

en·do·me·tri·o·sis (endō-mētrē-ōsr·do) noun, a condition resulting from the appearance of endometrial tissue outside the uterus and causing pelvic pain and infertility.

At first, I thought it wasn't as bad as it sounded. I knew deep in my heart I was meant to be a mother, and I would have my turn; it would just take a bit longer. And longer and longer and longer.

For fifteen years, I suffered from infertility. I endured three surgeries, four intrauterine inseminations, one in vitro fertilization (IVF), and two IVF transfers; I visited nine different doctors, went on five yoga retreats, fasted, did acupuncture, and even sought insight from a Sifu. What's a Sifu? Well, for me it was a man who charged us a small mortgage payment to roll around our living room floor because "a bear" had leapt into his body to deliver us a very important message as to why I could not conceive. His diagnosis? I was allergic to dog saliva.

I had made six embryos during my first IVF attempt. This meant I had six chances of becoming a mom, and that was it, as I did not take well to the drugs and the IVF process. They made me suicidal (which is not an exaggeration) and physically very sick.

Things I broke in fits of rage during my IVF cycle: a

remote control, a Lladró figurine, and two vases filled with flowers from Ryan.

And then finally, finally, I got pregnant, and then quickly, eighteen days later, I miscarried. And while I thought that was bad, I had no idea how bad it could actually get. A year later, I got the guts to try IVF again. I had used two embryos for my first attempt. I used two more embryos this time and voilà! I was pregnant. We named her Baby Maeby, because Maeby was the only guarantee we had when it came to this process, and we were also big *Arrested Development* fans.

Baby Maeby was ours for fourteen blissful weeks. I talked to her and played "The Rainbow Connection" on my phone, holding it next to my belly. I even allowed myself to look at possible themes for her nursery. Every night I prayed to just let her be okay, to keep her mine. Then one day, at a routine sonogram, I was told she was not okay, and less than twenty-four hours later, I was wheeled into an operating room for a forced DNC, strapped to the table, violently screaming and crying, "No, no, no!" until the drugs knocked me out. This destroyed me.

It happened a few weeks before Thanksgiving. We were not feeling festive and didn't want to ruin the holiday for the rest of my family, so when I told Ryan I didn't want to celebrate Thanksgiving that year, he quickly asked me, "Where do you want to go?" I responded, without hesitating, Spain. Why? I have no idea. It was a place I'd never been but always wanted to visit.

A week later we arrived in Barcelona. Sadly, there

wasn't enough *patatas bravas* or sangria in the city to make me smile, so we rented a car and drove with only one goal: to stop when we saw water.

We stumbled upon the town of Cadaqués. It was two nights before Thanksgiving. It was dark and cold. I felt a million miles away from my life back home. The next morning, I went for a hike by myself. I found an old church on top of a hill. It was empty. When I entered, I got down on my knees and just wept. Wept like I had never wept before. Anyone struggling with infertility knows how lonely it can be. How strong you become in order to cope. Well, in that small church I dropped the facade of all that strength. I spoke out loud to God, both surrendering to his plan but also, by using some choice words, demanding that he show me his plan already.

On the way back to the hotel, I saw a beautiful white house, directly on the water, with ornate art outside and one very large egg on the roof. I walked closer to check it out and saw a small group of about six people or so waiting patiently outside to enter.

It turned out to be Salvador Dalí's house, and people waited years to take a coveted tour of his home in Portlligat. I asked the tour guide if there was any chance we could visit during our stay, and lucky for us, one couple had backed out. They had an opening on Thanksgiving.

The next day, Ryan and I walked into Dalí's house. When I entered, I immediately started to feel better—the most okay I had felt in a while. When we got to the bedroom, I learned that Dalí's wife's name was Gala. I also learned quickly that these two, Dalí and Gala, were crazy (the fun kind of crazy), although they were broken in other ways. Imperfect. And there we were, Ryan and me, broken, on a day of perfect family traditions, inside the home of two others as perfectly imperfect as us. I turned to Ryan and said two things: one, if we ever have a little girl, I want to name her Gala, and two, I never again wanted to spend Thanksgiving away from home or our family.

And two years and two Thanksgivings later, with the last two embryos and the help of an incredibly loving family, our little girl, Gala Lee, was born via a surrogate. I still suffer from endometriosis, I will never know what it is like to carry my own child, and I still mourn for the three babies I lost (Gala was a twin). But when my tears well up and I start asking, "Why?" I remember that little seaside town and the house with the egg on its roof, nothing but a fishing village to some but to me the place where I was forever granted permission to be perfectly imperfect.

# Mazel Chow

The year I turned thirty, my best friend was thirty years my senior, and her name was Lee. We met in a nightclub while working on a party for the Rolling Stones. How's that for a name drop?

I had been in business for about a year when I received a call from Patti Hansen's manager (Patti, the gorgeous wife of Keith Richards), saying that they were looking for the hippest and coolest nightclub. I did my research and learned that a new club, The Pink Elephant, was soon to open and guaranteed to be the hottest and hardest-to-get ticket in town. (This was back when nightclubs actually existed in New York City. Thanks, Rudy.) It was perfect. I called and set up a meeting with a woman named Lee who was running the venue. She was chatty on our first call, like an instant friend, but then a little confused when I arrived for our meeting, as if it were the wrong day or even the wrong week. I'd later learn that Lee often had no idea what day it was, which grew to became one of her loveable charms.

Lee was someone that you met once and felt like you had known for years, or maybe in a past life. She put you at ease immediately, with either a funny joke or her infectious smile. With Lee, you were "in" from the moment you met. Inclusive and warm, she made you feel like you were part of her *mishpucha*. Nothing was off the table to discuss. If you were in, she would share it all with you.

"Well, you know, Mary, it was the sixties: everyone had herpes."

We spent about a month getting to know each other while preparing for the Stones. I learned some very important things that month: Mick Jagger was a vegetarian, Keith Richards only drank Sunkist soda and vodka, and, most importantly, Lee Blumer was the coolest person I'd ever met. By the time the party was over, I didn't want to be best friends with the Rolling Stones; I wanted to be best friends with Lee.

I remember the first date we made to hang after the Stones party. We went to see a movie and ate at a deli. Lee got a kick that I was an Italian girl who used Yiddish words, and I got a kick out of how she could talk and talk and talk and talk and talk, but it was never boring. If my Papa Charlie were around, he would say, "Lee could talk the ears off a field of corn."

She'd tell me stories about being hired to work

"security" at the first Woodstock in 1969 or working for Bill Graham and my beloved Monkees. I nearly fell to the ground when we made that connection, and she nearly fell to the ground when I told her what a crazy Monkees freak I was (rare for a girl who grew up in the 1980s). When I took her to see them at The Beacon (front row), she turned to me while I was in hysterical tears upon hearing "I'm a Believer" and said, "You weren't kidding." Once, we spent a whole New Year's Day in our pajamas: me, Ryan, Lee, and her friend Jim, listening with open mouths as Lee and Jim described their time in the Church of Scientology, where they met. Lee had jumped ship early; Jim made it onto "the boat."

I found myself looking forward to my time with Lee more than I did time with my contemporaries. Most of my pals were starting their families, and we had little in common. I had no interest in discussing their sleepless nights, and my gal pals didn't love things like listening to jazz all day on Sundays or catching a show at the Village Vanguard.

Years passed, and we grew closer. Lee was the same age as my mom, so it would be reasonable to assume that our relationship was like mother and daughter. But Lee wasn't a mother figure. My own mother filled that place. Lee came into my life at a time when I was struggling to become a mother, wanted nothing more than to be a mother. My longing made it hard for me to be around my own mom, as she felt my pain too deeply, and I grew angry that she, as my parent, could not fix what was broken.

Lee would urge me to be present and not dwell on what I did not have, and focus on what I did. She had gotten pregnant later in life and given birth to her son Alex, the love of her life. "It will happen when you're 40, just like me," she'd assure me. "You still have things to do. Until then, enjoy your life."

She made me laugh during a time when laughter in my life was sparse. She was the perfect mixture of kind and hilarious, and every day she'd share with me a new misadventure. She twice left her cat inside her kitchen cupboard all day. She got Mondays confused with Tuesdays; while battling cancer, she would leave her medical pot brownies in places she shouldn't. She accidentally dosed my elderly beagle, Stanley, not once but twice with her potent edibles. When she called, you didn't have to even say hello, because the moment she heard the connection click open, she would just start talking. "I told you it was just a matter of time before it happened." I usually had no idea what "it" was, but I didn't mind. I loved listening to Lee.

One summer, Lee decided she wanted to go to an ashram in the Catskills for a week. "Are you sure, Lee? No carbs, no sugar, no WiFi?"—three things Lee loved. "Mary, I'm an old hippie. I can do this."

Day two, I got a phone call. "Mary, get me out of here." So like Thelma, I jumped in my car, off to save my Louise.

I will never, ever forget pulling up and seeing Lee, standing on top of the hill, bags packed, ready, so ready to get the hell out of that place. I didn't even have time to shut off the car. She jumped in and said, "Hit it." I felt like the Blues Brothers as we peeled down the ashram's driveway.

We drove through the Catskill region, and she showed me the bungalow colony where she grew up and shared stories about the oddities of her childhood. She showed me the real Woodstock 1969 festival site and told me stories about the chaos. "It was truly just one big disaster site, but the most beautiful disaster the world had ever seen." We visited the Woodstock museum, and she took great pride in showing me her name, Lee Makler, displayed behind a glass in a case at the Museum at Bethel Woods at the site of the 1969 Woodstock Music and Arts Fair.

After our visit to the museum, Lee was hungry. She had just spent two whole days on the ashram, so where did we end up? In a kosher Chinese restaurant in Fallsburg, New York, named Mazel Chow. We laughed until we cried, eating wontons blessed by rabbis.

At sixty-eight, Lee was told she was dying. She was given four months to live. Lee's death was not an option for me; I would not accept it. I sent her to a last-resort homeopathic retreat in Florida, known to cure cancer with green juice and yoga. Again, she lasted two days and called me to say, "If I'm going to die, it's not going to be while I'm drinking green juice." She returned home, and I spent as much time as I could with her but also found myself moving away, trying to prepare, to wrap my head around the thought of her absence on this earth, which was simply too much for me to absorb.

She turned sixty-nine, a symbolic milestone we all hoped she'd make, ten days before she died. I helped organize her last birthday, running around the city that morning searching frantically for all the things I could fill her hospital room with that I hoped would make her smile. I cried all the way up Third Avenue holding colorful balloons with peace signs in one hand, a bouquet of Gerber daisies in the other. We celebrated her life that night and she was surrounded by the lucky ones who were blessed to call Lee their friend, too. One year later, almost to the day, our daughter, Gala Lee, was born, just a few months shy of my fortieth birthday.

My last email from the late great Lee Blumer:

> I'll miss your heart, you do so much, you
> give so much of your heart. I don't need
> much but for you to inspire.

## Mini Pastrami Spring Rolls

Though an hors d'oeuvre may seem like a silly way to remember my friend, one bite takes me back to Mazel Chow. Lee would have thought a pastrami-filled spring roll was weirdly delicious. Red Farm in New York City makes the best one.

### MAKES 24 PIECES

8 ounces pastrami (If you live in New York and have access to Katz's Delicatessen, go for it!)

¼ cup sauerkraut

2 tablespoons deli mustard

1 package wonton/spring roll wrappers (available in most grocery stores)

¼ cup all-purpose flour

1 cup water

½ cup cooking oil

......................................................

Mince pastrami, then combine with the sauerkraut and mustard in a bowl.

Whisk water and flour in another bowl and set aside.

Roll out 8 wontons, and place 1 tablespoon of pastrami filling horizontally in the center.

Wrap the pastry around the filling, and seal the rolls shut using a pastry brush to apply the flour mixture.

Heat oil in a skillet. There should be enough oil so the spring rolls swim in it to fry. Once oil is at 365°F, drop in spring rolls and fry until brown, 1 to 2 minutes each.

Place on a paper-towel-lined plate to cool.

Cut each roll into 4 small pieces and serve with mustard.

# Love and Marriage . . .
# and a Catering Company

When someone tells me that they want to quit their job and open a catering company because they love to entertain, I give them a little test. I ask them to imagine how it would feel to throw a party almost every day for an entire year. Now imagine throwing multiple parties on the same day. Next, I ask them how they feel about physical and mental exhaustion (often at the same time) and guests with endless complicated food allergies. Finally, I ask if, keeping all this in mind, they're prone to panic attacks.

The next thing to determine is whether the person is suffering from Hallmark Channel–caliber delusions of grandeur. Symptoms include believing that taking the plunge to hang up a catering shingle will be effortless and exciting and a quick road to success. A whirl of white tablecloths and sparkling crystal and—Whammo! Every day's a party.

A hottie you've just met in your glamorous new life will fall in love with you, and you'll buy a house together with a fancy kitchen, and you'll live happily ever after with hors d'oeuvres at every meal.

It's a lot like Bill Murray's advice about love and marriage. Don't just set a date and get married, he said. Take that person and travel around the world. Go to places that are hard to get to and hard to get out of. And if, when you land in JFK, you're still in love with that person, then get married at the airport.

My advice for those who want to be caterers would be similar: Prepare a dish that you think is truly the best thing you've ever made. Now hold that dish while you run around the Whitney Museum's marble floors in high heels for several hours. Smile brightly. Field calls on your cell phone from panicked event planners spread around the city, reporting that the champagne glasses did not arrive at the *Vogue* party or the desserts for the Cohens' wedding party are on their way to the seventh floor of Bergdorf instead of the synagogue. Now, here's the real zinger: imagine doing all of the above with your spouse. If, after all that, you still say, "I'll love it!" then yes, you should start a catering company.

I speak from experience, because after I spent three years working at my first catering job, enduring all of what I described above, one morning I looked at my husband and instead of asking him if we could run away to a small town to become goat farmers, I said, "We should start our own catering company."

Ryan and I had already been married for four years when we made the decision to leave our jobs, me at the catering company where I was working and Ryan at the real estate company where he was working, empty our bank account ($5,000), and start a catering company. It's easy to make a decision like this when you're young and you have nothing to lose.

What should we call it? "Mary Giuliani Catering & Events," Ryan said without thinking. I said, "Okay," also without thinking. Easy, right?

We turned our living room into an office; we printed out business cards on our printer, and I decorated them with food illustrations from Kate's Paperie.

The Tribeca Film Festival was the first client to call, asking if we could cater fifteen parties during the course of one week. "Yes, we can," I said without even knowing whether it was true, and Mary Giuliani went from idea to real business.

We had a chef who cooked the food out of his kitchen in Connecticut and drove it into New York for the parties. We would meet him with our Jeep packed to the brim with beverages, party trays, decor items like candles and lanterns, and sometimes our dog, Stanley.

Our roles emerged quickly. I was the balloon left to fly freely and create, and Ryan was the rock that tethered my balloon to Earth, pulling me back when I started to drift too far.

We made a deal that when we felt the business was

affecting our marriage, each of us reserved the right to push the stop button and walk away. We made a promise to each other that we came first, the business second. We never expected our business to grow as quickly as it did. One day we woke up and realized the business was affecting our marriage, but we were both too far in, with too much at stake, to press stop like we had promised each other. Throw fifteen years of infertility on top of all of that, and man oh man, is life anything but a party.

I married Ryan because I truly loved him in the deepest way I had ever loved anything before in my life (this includes the Monkees, pasta carbonara, and cheese fries). We met after college, working at the same restaurant in East Hampton, I as a hostess and he as a long-haired waiter/bartender. On our first date, we played a game of darts and drank a beer, and when I arrived home that night, my mother answered the door asking me, "DID YOU HEAR!?" I responded, "What? That I just had a date with the man I'm going to marry?" And she said, "No! Princess Diana died."

We got married on the beach in Montauk, and love became our focus. But marriage isn't all about love for each other. It's about love for your career, for your individual goals, for your goals as a couple. Any time I've noticed Ryan unhappy about where he was in his life, I've stopped and asked him what, to me, was always a simple and targeted question: "Do you love what you're doing?" A few times, the answer was no, and he changed his career with my support. He has done the same for me. Ryan gives me the freedom to be me, with no boundaries. I dream and plan and love to the fullest extent of my being, and it keeps me creative. It may sound silly, but I fall in love every day: with men, women, cities, TV shows, clothing designers, animals, you name it. I once asked Ryan if he was okay with this, and he answered, "As long as you always love me the most."

Giving each other the openness to dream helped us realize that it was time for him to walk away from the dream he helped me achieve, and I was to move into the role of his supporter as he left the catering company to open a restaurant and hotel in Woodstock. True love allows you to drift and dream and create, and delights in the space that allows you to become fulfilled. John and Yoko were onto something with those "lost weekends."

So, should you start a catering company or any other business that appeals to your passion, and even more importantly, should you do it with your spouse? As an attempt to answer, let me share what I have for years referred to as the Goldfish Shit story.

A few months after opening Mary Giuliani Catering & Events, I came up with what I felt was a genius idea: to serve food on trays engineered to be filled with water and live fish swimming around inside—essentially, goldfish bowls as flattish rectangular serving trays. Ryan balked, and we had our first big blowout over creative differences. I was adamant: this was an incredible idea that would be talked about in the catering world for years to come. He pushed and pushed me to change my mind, so much so that I told him he should not even come to the party.

About an hour into the party at the Ferragamo store on Fifth Avenue, the fish, petrified to be swimming around in a tray covered in crab cakes and mini burgers and carried through a crowded party, began shitting and having heart attacks (if goldfish have heart attacks) and dying. Disaster. Client upset, party fail.

When I got home that night and got into bed, I told Ryan the story, and instead of saying, "I told you so," or being angry that we lost a big client over my crazy idea, he started to laugh, and I started to laugh, and that's when I knew I was going to fall asleep and wake up in the arms of my husband, not my business partner. And that felt great.

# Things I'm Looking Forward to Teaching My Daughter

The Monkees are the single-most underrated band in
America.

Rip Taylor was an America treasure.

You will never regret *not* going forward with that
Brazilian wax. (I tried it once. After Sue completed
the right side, I sat up, screamed, "Why the hell
would anyone do this?" and left the waxing room
as a porn star on the left, 1960s activist on the
right.)

If you don't like your job, quit. Life is too short to
be spent in a cubicle, wearing headgear, in a place
where you see no future. Just don't quit your job

by going to lunch and not coming back. They *will* call your mother (like they did mine), and she will think you're dead, floating in the Hudson River, instead of at a matinee screening of *The Notebook*.

Don't assume people are nice just because they're vegans.

Don't be overly generous. My dear, late friend Lee, your namesake, told me that generosity is mistaken for weakness, and if you're like your mama, you will learn more than one difficult lesson that proves this to be true. Generosity extended for the wrong reasons—to make people like you, to win friends, to placate an aggressor—is chewed up and quickly forgotten. Generosity should always be motivated by love, not fear or insecurity.

Something for nothing is nothing! Do not work for free. Don't be so trusting in business: I have learned this the hard way. Don't say yes to people in power just because they have power. Have skin in the game, get a good lawyer, and fight like a big girl for what is yours.

Don't google yourself more than once a week.

Don't think the bigger house is, by default the better house.

Love first, think second.

# Lady Lobsters

Most of my true educational milestones have come from watching television. It will come as no surprise to you that I was an avid fan of the TV show *The Monkees*. One show in particular, an episode in which Frank Zappa guest-starred, served as a vocabulary lesson when he used the words *banal* and *insipid* to describe the Monkees' music. (I had no idea this was an insult until after I pulled out the old *Webster's*.) When "banal" appeared on my SAT, I had Frank Zappa to thank for getting that one correct. As I grew up in a strict Catholic household, everything I learned about sex was the direct result of too much time in front of the TV. I thought everyone kissed like the actors on my grandmother's soap operas. And HBO's airing of *Revenge of the Nerds* literally rocked my world. I have spent half of my postpubescent life waiting to make out with someone named Stan in a Darth

Vader mask on one of those blow-up bouncy space things.

Where am I going with this? Well, a few years ago, I was watching *The L Word*—yes, the show that encouraged me to cut my hair into the perfect Sally Hershberger shag and start wearing more leather. On one episode of *The L Word*, the ladies are together at dinner, and one tells the group that when male lobsters get tossed into a pot, they build a ladder to help each other try to escape, but female lobsters actually pull each other down, dragging everyone to the bottom so they can all die together. Now, for the record, I have no idea if this is a scientific fact (the internet reveals a total mishmash of conflicting opinions from everyone except experts in crustacean circles). However, I will tell you that this forced me to think about my female relationships in a different way.

I started to observe my female friendships more closely, as well as look back at friendships from the past. Clearly I had occasionally been in the proverbial pot with other lady lobsters. Did the theory hold? If I was honest with myself, I had at times not behaved like a very good lady lobster myself, giving in to petty gossip and "pulling down" others at girls' dinners and outings. The relationships built on this type of "camaraderie" did not feel like places I wanted to be anymore.

I also started to think about my career and realized that I could count on two hands the number of highly successful men who had helped me in business, and I didn't even need five fingers to tally the number of women. Huge lobster claw applause for Rachael Ray for being an exception to the lady lobster rule. Unthreatened by other women's success, Rachael has invited me on her show to celebrate my hard work and creativity. She has joyfully shared her stage with me, and her acts of kindness to me have been wholly unselfish. She truly wants me to succeed. Perhaps women who've achieved success by remaining true to themselves are able to pay it forward.

I then thought about the lady lobsters from whom I hail: my grandmother Lucille was a maverick entrepreneur and a business badass in the 1960s. At a time when women were just supposed to look pretty and perform such vital tasks as hollowing out watermelons for Jell-O molds, Lucille was a pioneer, carving out a new life for herself in the then unknown town of Montauk, creating an empire while wearing a pantsuit! I know members of my own family just shook their heads at her "crazy idea" of opening a resort and becoming an independent woman to be reckoned with. I can only imagine the harsh lady lobster treatment she endured because she "clawed" her way down her own path (and out of that damned pot!).

I have endured some big ups and downs in the company of my own posse of lady lobsters. I've had fantastic business successes and spectacular failures. My excruciating, long struggle with infertility caused by endometriosis (and my personal diagnosis: too many martinis) happily ended with me welcoming my baby girl into this world. And through this, I realized that the best lady lobster to share your pot with is, yes, the one who is right there beside you on your hardest day but, as importantly, is also there for you on your best day. That friend who looks you in the eyes and tells you she is proud of you, and you believe her because she, too, is crying with joy after hearing that Micky Dolenz responded to your fan letter, and she doesn't even like the Monkees.

I chose to become a kinder lobster, to listen more to the needs of my friends, and to encourage rather than to pull apart. It is so much easier to build people up and support them than it is to pull them down, and the more I began to do that, the more I saw and felt kind actions bestowed upon me by other lady lobsters. I even began to meet amazing lobsters whom I don't think I would have come across if I stayed pot-locked in my old habits.

What kind of lobster are you? What kind of lobsters are in your pot? I think if we all pause and amp up the kindness to each other, we may just make it up that ladder and not end up on a plate next to the coleslaw.

# Mini Lobster Rolls

MAKES 24 ROLLS

3 lobsters, 1¼ pounds each

1 cup kosher salt

1 lemon, cut in half

3 fresh bay leaves

1 English cucumber, peeled, seeded, and ¼-inch-diced

2 tablespoons mayonnaise

¼ cup crème fraîche or sour cream

2 teaspoons each of fresh tarragon, chives,
and chervil, all chopped fine and combined

Zest and juice of 1 lemon

1 teaspoon Old Bay seasoning

½ teaspoon Tabasco hot sauce

Kosher salt and black pepper, to taste

1 bunch watercress picked, cleaned, and dried

2 dozen 2-inch mini hot dog brioche buns

¼ cup butter, melted

..........................................................

Fill a large pot three-quarters full with water and bring to a boil.

Add about a cup of kosher salt, one lemon cut in half, and 3 fresh bay leaves. Simmer for about 5 minutes to infuse the flavors.

While the water is getting ready, on a cutting board, take a large chef's knife and drive it through the center of each lobster head, about an inch behind the eyes, killing the lobster instantly.

When the water is ready, carefully add the lobsters to the water and simmer until cooked through, about 10 minutes.

Remove the lobsters and allow to drain and cool for about 15 minutes before attempting to crack the shells and remove the tail, claw, and knuckle meat. Cut the meat into small chunks and place in a medium-sized bowl.

Recipe continues on next page

..............................................

Add the cucumber, mayonnaise, crème fraîche, 4 teaspoons of herbs, lemon, Old Bay, and Tabasco. Gently stir to combine; taste and adjust with salt and pepper.

Preheat oven to 350°F and put a medium nonstick sauté pan on a low flame.

Split each mini hot dog brioche bun down the middle halfway through. Open the buns to expose the center, brush with butter, and place in the sauté pan to lightly brown. Then place on a cookie sheet. Repeat until complete.

Place the tray in the oven for about 3 minutes to heat the bread throughout. Spread watercress leaves across each bun, followed by a generous mound of the lobster salad, and garnish with additional 2 teaspoons of chopped herbs.

# Private Planes

"I'm flying high over Tupelo, Mississippi, with
America's hottest band and we're all about to die."

—William Miller, in *Almost Famous*

This is pretty much exactly what happened the first time I
took a private plane. Ryan and I had been in Los Angeles
for an extended stay. We spent the day drinking poolside
at our home-away-from-home, the Sunset Marquis, with a
few old and new friends, one being a capital B Bold-Faced
Name, who leaned in to ask us a question. "How do the
Giulianis get home from L.A.?" said one of the most recognizable celebrities of the day.

"Jet Blue. Red eye." I responded.

"Not tomorrow." He handed his phone to Ryan and

commanded, "Put your name, date of birth, and driver's license number in my phone. I'm adding you to the passenger list. We leave at 7 a.m. See you tomorrow." And he walked off.

I, of course, knew how private air travel worked, but these invites never came flying our way. Once, when I was working for the entertainment agency, I heard one of the managers say how lucky he was to "hop a flight back with Keanu after Sundance," and while refilling a cheese platter for a socialite, I overheard her saying, "I can always hop on so-and-so's plane back from St. Barths if I get bored." That's a lot of hopping! But us? No one had ever asked us to hop aboard on a whim.

But instead of being excited about this potentially once-in-a-lifetime proposition, I was terrified. I spent the next twelve hours weighing the pros and cons of turning down this invite and googling private plane crash statistics. I even called my mother (a mistake: she's even more terrified of air travel than I am), who took the opportunity to remind me once again how JFK Jr. had died.

I asked Ryan if we could politely decline, but he was having none of it. He was very excited to get this invite and to "hop aboard." He told me to have a drink before we went and that we'd kick back and enjoy the ride. I followed his advice. I had three before stumbling into the hotel lobby at 7 a.m. Lucky for me, we had visited with the owner of a tequila company on our trip, who gifted us three very expensive bottles of DeLeón tequila. My trip home was sponsored by DeLeón and half a Xanax.

When our host showed up downstairs, he looked as if he had forgotten that he had invited us, but he shook off his own hangover, cleared away the memory cobwebs, pointed to the door, and barked, "Let's go!"

Outside the Sunset Marquis, a car pulled up, and out stepped one more of the most recognizable celebrities of our time. Think big!

"You're late," our host told this mega celeb, who apologized and made a joke. And then off we went! Me and Ryan and two of the biggest names you've ever heard, in a black SUV, tearing down Sunset Boulevard, with Led Zeppelin blaring as we headed to Van Nuys Airport. What was happening?

When the gate to the tarmac opened and our car continued driving right to the open door of the ginormous private plane we were taking home, my fear turned to excitement with a dash of tequila joy, and I decided to embrace this moment. Carpe diem! I guess.

The two pilots were waiting at the foot of the airplane stairs with big smiles and open arms. I followed the two celebs and Ryan up, stepping onto the plane with my right foot (one of my many superstitious Sicilian rituals). Once aboard, I saw a food buffet as abundant as brunch at the Ritz-Carlton spread out before us: bagels, schmears, fruit, lox, and a full bar (thank God) containing every type of booze or beverage known to man.

Once the plane door locked shut, I clung to my now

fourth drink, and as we took off to Sinatra's "Come Fly with Me" played in the soundtrack of my mind. I was literally and figuratively flying.

What's it like? Well, in one word, amazing. No TSA; no demonstration of that terrifying yellow life vest, pulling the cord to inflate, with an equally horrifying safety video playing on the seat-back monitors (because come on, gang, no one is smiling when they are sliding down that emergency wing slide); no constant reminders about seat belts, on and off, on and off; no reused airplane pillows or blankets; no disgruntled stewardesses (in fact, the stewardess was so accommodating, I felt if I asked her to have a Trans Am with Burt Reynolds waiting for us when we landed in New York, she would have said, "Certainly," with a smile).

Halfway thought the flight, I had calmed down and settled into what was clearly to be my new travel lifestyle, even cracking up the whole plane by saying out loud to Ryan, "Remember, honey, when we used to fly commercial?"

Drinks flowed, laughter abounded—this was amazing. What had I been so worried about? Until the bumps. And not just those cute little turbulence bumps that make you think about being generous to your seatmate and sharing your armrest, offering to hold his or her hand. No, this turbulence made you contemplate whether or not you'd been a kind person, as heaven or hell was clearly your next stop.

And the bumpy ride didn't let up: an entire planeload of men, along with me and the stewardess (strangely, the only women), sat in silence, white knuckling our way through what we learned later was a massive Nor'easter that had closed Newark, JFK, LaGuardia, and now Teterboro, where we were scheduled to land.

The pilot came out (uh-oh) to tell us to fasten our seat belts and that we were being diverted to Westchester. Our host pressed him on this: "Let's try for Teterboro." Ever my mother's daughter, I was reminded of an article I had read in *Vanity Fair* stating that most private plane accidents happen because of ego. Every part of my body was sweating: ego was going to kill us, every one of us!

Ironically, one passenger on our plane was actually in the movie *Almost Famous*, in that pivotal scene when the characters are on board a plane that is about to go down, with everyone making spontaneous announcements, like "I've always loved so-and-so" or "I'm gay." I'm a believer in life imitating art, but this was way too much.

In between Hail Marys, Our Fathers, and passages from the Torah I had memorized during my attempt to be Jewish, I started to imagine the headlines. Would Ryan and I make the front page with these two luminaries? Or would we simply be the "other passengers"? Maybe not front page, but maybe second? Who else died with Buddy Holly and Ritchie Valens, and what was their billing in the coverage?

Then it was time. Not one, not two, but three attempted landings, meaning the plane went down and back up *three* times.

Finally, after I made several deals with God, including sticking to the no-meat-on-Fridays-during-Lent rule (sausage on your pizza does in fact count), we landed at Teterboro. I never saw a group of people run off a plane faster. I think one of these superstars—certainly no stranger to private air travel—ran to the bathroom to puke, because when he joined us outside the airport to wait for our cars, he was green.

Ryan likes to say that I exaggerate, but even he was firmly in agreement that the Giulianis had tried their hand at "hopping aboard" and from then on preferred to fly the friendly skies with the masses and the terrible blow-up vests and the smiling actors on the video screens. Jet Blue, not jet set, is the life for me.

# Laughing in Her Sleep

One night, while wrestling with insomnia caused by my impending book deadline (yes, this book), Gala, then three years old and, yes, still in our bed, let out the most delightful toddler giggle in her sleep. If you've never heard a child laugh in her sleep, you're missing something great.

When you are preparing to become a new mom, people love to share all the joys that await you. They tell you how your life will change for the better. How it's hard in the beginning, but then one day your little son or daughter will grab your face and say, "I love you," for the first time and your world with be forever altered. I awaited all these beautiful milestones, but the one thing that no one prepared me for, that truly knocked my socks off (does that ever really happen?), was her first sleep giggle.

The first time Gala laughed in her sleep, she was

snuggled tightly on my chest, which is where she spent a good twelve to fifteen hours a day during the first three months of her life. I made the decision to have as much skin-to-skin with my little miracle as I possibly could, based on the facts that (a) I had waited fifteen long years for her to arrive, and (b) since I did not carry her in my womb, this was our very special "get to know each other" time.

So there she was, snuggled next to my heart, and while I did something important, like stalk Justin Theroux's Instagram feed or order a T-shirt that says SHIRT HAPPENS on Amazon, much to my surprise, she let out a tiny baby giggle. Startled at first, wondering if I'd heard what I thought I'd heard, I stared at her intensely for a few minutes. Sure enough, she let out another little giggle, accompanied by one of those little spastic arm movements that make you google "What is wrong with my baby?" For the record, I googled so many things when she was a baby that I wore out the G button on my laptop. I then googled "Why do babies laugh in their sleep?" According to the experts on the internet, the reason is not entirely clear. No one knows if they dream, but surely they might. I began to endlessly obsess over what she was dreaming about. What was making her laugh? Was Don Rickles doing a tiny little show just for her? Did she see a group of unicorns smelling their own farts? Or was my little girl comedically gifted?

Just in case my daughter was endowed with a super-sized sense of humor, I started Gala on a heavy dose of old episodes of *SNL* (1975 and 1976 seasons only), *SCTV*, and

Joan Rivers, along with *Baby Einstein* and *Sesame Street*. That tiny baby giggle kicked off my parenting style in a big way. Comedy was to be our thing. It steers my parental decision making, from angry to silly, so that when I want to scream or lose my patience, I break into Gilda Radner's Roseanne Roseannadanna or Steve Martin's "King Tut" dance, which, I am proud to say, Gala can perform like a boss.

She's been John Belushi for two of her three Halloweens on Earth (Belushi Bee and a Blues Brother). We're working on Samurai Belushi for next year, but she doesn't seem to be taking to those skits in the way I had hoped.

Yes, yes, I'm teaching her kindness and manners and the ABCs, but as importantly, I'm teaching her the value of finding laughter in the good times and the bad. God knows, it has helped me navigate some pretty tricky spots from my childhood until today.

Will knowing the entire opening monologue of *Blazing Saddles* get her into Harvard? Who knows, but also who cares? As long as my kid keeps laughing either on the subway or in her sleep, then I'll give myself two stars and a pat on the back for a job well done.

# Goodnight, Goodman

"Someone suggested that there's an incomplete
part of our chromosomes that gets repaired
or found when we hit New Orleans.
Some of us just belong here."

—John Goodman

When you plan creative escapes for other people for a living (which is another way to describe event planning), it is imperative that you yourself find a place where you can go to escape creatively for a while. This is a place that forces you to forget who you are, what you do, and to whom you belong and allows you to totally immerse yourself in the culture and the lifestyle of somewhere new for a while. For me, the year I turned thirty-three, New Orleans became this escape, almost before the plane landed.

It's the one city in which I can drop my bags and forget to unpack for days. I cannot hit the street fast enough, not caring that the humidity is so thick, I get an instantaneous frizzy new 'do, which is not my best look. The first sound of a brass band or sight of a cypress tree ignites my soul, bad hair and all.

New Orleans is also the one place I have ever been where I felt like I belonged, which is pretty hilarious considering I'm as New York as they come and never spent any time in the South, unless of course you count South Florida. But something mystical and magical puts me at ease immediately. Everything just feels right.

My first trip to New Orleans was in honor of my dearest friend, Lydia Fenet's wedding. I checked into my hotel and met her in Jackson Square so that she could show me her New Orleans. We embraced, and I declared with certainty that while I may be an Italian New Yorker, I felt like I was home. I should reveal that all I knew about New Orleans prior to Lydia's wedding weekend came from my very deep crush on the actor John Goodman. Goodman lived in New Orleans and spoke often and passionately about his beloved Crescent City. I'd always investigate restaurants or bars he mentioned frequenting in hopes of crossing paths with him. Ever since the first episode of *Roseanne*, I've found Goodman to be quite dreamy. And speaking of dreams, I should also confess the following: I've had reoccurring dreams about John Goodman for years. Not sexy dreams (although I'm not opposed to a little JG nocturnal visit) but ones in which we see each other at the supermarket and say hi or find ourselves in the same pew at church and shake hands during the peace offering. Familiar. Comforting. Even more curiously, he's the only person I've ever had recurring dreams about. I've seen all his films (even the random ones, like *Arachnophobia*). *Sea of Love* stands out as one of my early favorites, but the one that really made me fall deeply in love was *Everybody's All-American*. Let's face it, because I'm fine with it: I'm a sucker for a big guy, and don't even get me started on the magnificence that is Goodman in any Coen brothers' film.

But sadly, not one trip to New Orleans has ever yielded a Goodman sighting. And I'd be lying if I told you I wasn't strongly willing one every single time I'm there. Once, when I was in town for a food charity event and was told he might be joining the after-party dinner, my little heart broke so deeply when his seat remained empty all night that I ate almost an entire king cake and didn't even care if I choked on the little plastic baby. This city and John Goodman are one for me.

I've spent nights in New Orleans with some of the most inspiring people on the planet. Rock stars in the music world and rock stars in the kitchen. I was very fortunate to be part of an annual expedition to New Orleans with a motley gang of chefs. We would arrive from New York to alight in the city, eating, drinking, and dancing our way to euphoric heights (except for the time Ryan ended up in urgent care with a diagnosis of too much shellfish and

Sazerac). One year, on the plane ride home from one such trip, I sat happily among a group of deeply hungover and dehydrated food lunatics, all dreaming of "just getting home," with whom I had just shared three long New Orleans daze. I thought about how lucky we were to escape our lives for a just a few moments—that a city exists just to delight us so much that we can return to the mundane tasks of daily life with renewed inspiration and appreciation. I'm so grateful for those trips, which I've shared with the funny fishmonger, the pastry goddess, the singing chef, the ice cream maker, the caterer, the tapas masters, and three of the best *caccio e peppe* makers in the world.

Back to Goodman. A few months ago, I had one of my reoccurring Goodman dreams. I couldn't remember the context; I just woke up and headed straight for my computer. New Orleans was pulling me by my hair again. My book deadline was a month away, and I was going to spend the last week in New Orleans finishing it, creating my new ritual there, like James Caan's character in *Misery*, when he finishes a novel by pouring himself a glass of the same wine and lighting a cigarette.

Without hesitating, I booked a pink house with a pool through Airbnb for a week—without reading the reviews, without talking to my husband. Two weeks later, we were on our way. When we arrived, the house was as special and delightful as the pictures suggested. Relief. The hosts were incredible and greeted us with the warmest of southern welcomes, which was a beautiful BBQ with drinks and instant new friends, people who remain my New Orleans friends. While sitting in their incredible parlor dining room, surrounded by art and playing the New Orleans alphabet game (I learned that a rat in New Orleans is called a nutria), I asked the one question I ask of everybody who makes their home in New Orleans: does John Goodman really live here?

"Live here? He lives right there." One of the guests, a neighbor, responded, pulling back the curtains to reveal that Goodman's house was literally right across the street from my little guest cottage, the one I blindly booked after he appeared in my dream. I tried to play it cool, as I didn't want to startle these lovely people with my sudden joy and excitement, but secretly I was dying inside. Goodman was right across the street.

After dinner, we headed up to our house, and after getting Gala down to sleep, I set up my computer on the terrace, my newly christened writing desk looking directly into what I decided was John Goodman's bedroom because it was the only room in the house in which a small light burned. Naturally, I decided it was the light next to Goodman's bed and that he was there, maybe reading, maybe watching SportsCenter, maybe clipping his toe nails. I looked down at my computer and got lost in my words. At around midnight, when the small light across the street went out, I looked up and whispered, "Goodnight, Goodman."

The next day was really just an exercise in waiting for Gala to fall asleep again so I could open my computer again and spend some creative evening hours with Goodman. I truly cannot describe how much joy I felt in seeing his light on again. The lamp. Goodman's lamp. I got lost again in my words. Hours went by, and then the light switched off as it had the night before. "Goodnight, Goodman."

This ritual continued for the seven nights we spent in New Orleans. Each night, I stopped when his light went out, and I too headed off to bed, as though John were signaling me that it was time to turn in so that the spirits of New Orleans could fill my head with more inspiration while I slept.

It was one of the most productive writing weeks I'd ever had. The last night before I was heading back to New York, I sat at my desk, putting the finishing touches on the manuscript. Even my final-night edits seemed to flow easily, guided by the light coming from Goodman's bedside lamp. For the first time, I looked at the clock the moment the light went out. Slowly, as if waking from a nap on a hot New Orleans summer day, I realized that the light had gone out at the same time every night. A timer, not Goodman, was signaling me to slumber. I learned on my way to the airport that he had not even been in residence in New Orleans while I finished my book, guided by his divine inspiration. He was off on some exotic vacation.

But hey, if my book ends up as something more than just a little present for my mother to hand out as Christmas gifts to all her friends, I'll be able to say, "Kerouac had Cassady. Fitzgerald had Zelda. Me? John Goodman's timer."

# Free HBO

The living room of our small cottage on Old Montauk Highway was illuminated only by the thirteen-inch-color television. While Johnny Carson interviewed Jack Hanna, my cousin Scott and I stole impatient glances at Papa Charlie lying on the floor, his black leather shoe under his head as pillow, a Kent cigarette dangling out of the corner of his mouth. I'd stare at his eyes as they fluttered opened and closed until finally they remained closed and the loud snores began.

Scott watched the window and signaled that the coast was clear. Slowly we rose from the couch and tiptoed past Papa, now definitely fast asleep on the floor. Scott's blond hair blew back in the wind as he silently and expertly slid open the glass door. As usual, I kneeled down and kissed Papa on his head—which drove Scott nuts but assuaged my guilt about my wrongdoing—pausing to make sure he was still snoring before moving toward the door. *Slide. Click.* We were free. Grandma Lucille's house twinkled before us, lit up with chandeliers and slightly drunk party guests. I loved Saturday nights.

. . .

In 1938, shortly after a big hurricane had swept through Montauk, Lucille had taken a train with her mother from Jamaica Avenue in Queens to Montauk, after seeing an ad in the Long Island Press for land for sale. Once there, Lucille purchased one plot of land for $100, her mother bought a few more, and the women together decided that their families would build their vacation homes there.

Lucille, bright and educated (the first woman in her family to attend college), had a certain fire, a restlessness that I understand all too well, that made her stand out from the rest. She married my grandfather Franklin, and they settled in Ozone Park, Queens. Her first son, Richard, was born in 1940, and then my father, Robert, came along in 1942 , then almost eighteen years later, her daughter Therese. Lucille was a piano teacher, and Franklin was an engineer at John Adams High School. The house was small for four people. Each time a plane took off or landed, the cabinets rumbled. It was unkempt and cluttered. Lucille was many things, but a 1950s housewife she was not. She loved her sons but was never fulfilled by motherhood in the way she was told she would be. Still, she threw herself into making sure that her sons took their studies seriously and succeeded, and she pushed them to dream big.

In the summer of 1947, Lucille and Franklin decided it was time to build their home in Montauk on that plot of land. Once the house was completed and all the work was done, there was no turning back. Lucille had grown even more deeply in love with Montauk and began to dream of ways to stay in this world, not the one waiting for her back in Queens.

In 1950, when my father was nine years old, he was in town with Lucille when a minor event changed their collective lives. In Clarence's grocery store, they overhead a visiting doctor ask Clarence if he knew of any places to stay. Desperate, the doctor offered Clarence $25 for the night for a place to stay for his wife and baby. That was all Lucille needed to hear. A light went on in her head, and Lucille offered him a stay in her newly built vacation home. My father recalls that she asked him and his brother to remove all their belongings from their bedroom, then set about changing the sheets and straightening up so that the doctor and his family could spend the night. They would be the first of thousands of guests Lucille would welcome to Montauk.

A business was born. With $11,000 loaned to her by her father, Lucille purchased a larger parcel of land in the center of town to build a hotel with twenty rooms, which she called The Wavecrest. The rooms would be laid out in the shape of an *L* for "Lucille." She would spend hours sitting on a folding metal chair outside the rooms, waving in customers. Little by little the business grew, and Lucille moved away from the role of wife and mother in the traditional sense of that era. She became more successful, and her can-do attitude continued to propel her to dream bigger, achieve more, set new goals for herself. In 1956, the same gentleman who sold Lucille and her mother their first pieces of land tempted Lucille with six oceanfront acres on the Montauk Highway. Lucille's crowning achievement, The Wavecrest on the Ocean, was born. It was a true resort with one hundred rooms, an indoor pool, a cocktail lounge named The Sea Witch, and later, during my childhood, the ever so coveted amenity of that era . . . FREE HBO.

The Wavecrest was our summer home for the first ten years of my life. It sat twenty-five feet from the edge of the Atlantic Ocean, the first resort you saw after the WELCOME TO MONTAUK sign, when the Old Montauk Highway forks right toward the ocean. My family of four (sometimes six, when my other grandparents came to stay) spent our time in one small, six-hundred-square-foot cottage. From the bedroom window, I would look up at Grandma Lucille's house, an octagonal, white castle-like structure that she had custom-built to sit high above her resort so that she could look out over her five acres of oceanfront land from the wraparound terrace.

It was a house built for parties, and Lucille was the ultimate entertainer. Specially selected hotel guests would receive a coveted invite to her weekend bacchanals, and

Lucille did not disappoint. She had a brand-new European kitchen and a cook and served three-course dinners. Lucille would play a baby grand piano that once belonged to Guy Lombardo to the delight of her guests, who would sing along drunkenly. The circular living/dining room boasted a 360-degree view of the ocean, and the fireplace was so enormous that it took up half the house. Lucille even had a moat built around the castle, filled with expensive koi. And if the moat wasn't over the top, my grandmother even had her very own glass elevator.

I never saw Grandma Lucille during the day. I would spend most of my day hoping for a glimpse, or even better, a conversation. I might catch her in the office below the castle in the late afternoons, instructing her many employees on how to properly greet the new guests when they arrived for the weekend, or I might sight her quickly as she jumped into the back of her brand-new Cadillac. But never once did I see her on the beach. I always found it odd, and maybe even a little sad, that a woman who had sacrificed her whole life to build an empire on the sea never once stepped foot on the sand.

In the rare moments I did catch her attention, I knew I would only hold it briefly, so I always tried to get in everything I wanted to tell her all at once, as if she were a celebrity (because, to me, she was) and I had those fabled fifteen seconds to pitch her a story. I remember practicing and outlining what I would say to Lucille, once opportunity struck. And just as when you're about five seconds into your pitch with many celebrities and you can see you've lost their attention, that's what it was like talking to Lucille.

Dinnertime on the weekends at The Wavecrest was always spent in our cottage with my family: Mom, Dad, my sister Nanette, Grandma Mary, and Papa Charlie. Most Saturdays, after dinner, my very handsome and very dressed-up father would drag my very beautiful dressed-up mother up to Lucille's castle for what he swore was "one last time" every weekend. Reluctant, she would allow herself to be dragged. She'd kiss us goodbye, leaving the smell of her Norell perfume on my sweatshirt.

I was aware at an early age of the tepid affection that existed between my parents and Lucille without truly understanding their history. With mom's kiss, I felt her reluctance to join in the weekend revelry, every time. The mystery of Grandma Lucille's parties, which my parents clearly did not want me to experience, made crashing them my most singular thought.

Lucille went on to become one of the largest landowners in Montauk, and by 1983, she owned three large hotels, full blocks of commercial real estate in the center of town, various homes spread out in different neighborhoods, and the ferry rights from Montauk to Block Island. She became known as an eccentric who lived in a tower and threw legendary parties. In short, she was a local celebrity and beloved by many but also became known as a hard, brash businesswoman, of whom I once heard a guest say, "She works like a man." I knew, even at a young age, that this was meant as an insult. Whoever said it didn't know how hard she worked, how alone she must have felt, how much she had to sacrifice only to be resented or have her success thrown in her face.

. . .

My cousin Scott and I snuck out of the cottage many times, but one night I remember distinctly. On this night, once we were out, I noticed that the circular driveway that wound its way up to The Wavecrest was packed with fancy cars, a sign that it was a good night to storm the fortress.

We walked past the vending machine that Scott had rigged to push out free Cokes. We grabbed a soda and hid behind a tree. I remember drinking the Coke, pretending I was slugging down a beer, delighting in doing something bad. With caffeine-fueled bravado, we soundlessly entered the castle, and the roar of music, combined with the smell of salt air and cigarettes, sent tingles up and down my spine. As I made my way up the circular staircase, the music was loud and clumsy, and by the tenth stair, the soundtrack had switched to something by Caruso, I think. With Grandma Lucille, you never knew what was coming next—another of her admirable charms, I thought.

When I finally reached the top, I opened the door and slowly peeked my head into the room from the hallway. Everything came at me like waves crashing on the shore. Smoke clouded the air from cigarettes and pipes; there were two men dancing with two other men, a belly dancer gyrating her hips to the music, lost in her own reverie, an Asian woman dancing with my grandmother's live-in tarot card reader (yes, you read that correctly), chaos and confusion so grand that I found it beyond invigorating—I found it literally intoxicating. And the outfits—everyone was so dressed up. Some of the same people I saw padding around in their bathing suits during the day were red-carpet-ready now. Everyone brought out the big guns for a night at Lucille's.

Out of this delicious chaos, like a record skipping and the needle landing on the perfect track, Lucille appeared, and the room paused for a moment. Lucille wasn't a traditional beauty, but she lit up a room when she walked into it; she had the presence of a movie star who knew she wasn't just today's flavor of month. She was wearing a purple silk dress with kimono sleeves that flared like wings, fake diamonds draped around her neck and running up and down her arms, a glass of wine in hand, and she made an announcement. She was going to play the piano.

The crowd roared and cheered her on, upping the madness. Everyone was lit, but it wouldn't have mattered because she was the master puppeteer and they were her puppets. And what a crew this was. A collection that included burly local fisherman, buttoned-up-by-week stockbrokers, celebrities, musicians, writers, and artists, maybe a lone priest or monsignor. You name it, they all wanted in on Grandma Lucille's parties.

She started playing the piano, and her audience cheered her on, screaming for more. People were losing their minds, yelling and cheering and wildly applauding. This was Lucille's show.

She was halfway through her song when she spotted me under a small skirted cocktail table, so enrapt that I dared to peek out and accidentally "outed" myself. We locked eyes, and my heart nearly stopped. But instead of drawing attention to me or ratting me out to my parents, she simply looked me right in the eye, winked, and carried on with her act. Somehow I knew that she was proud of me that I had the courage to defy my parents, to test boundaries, to storm her fortress. She saw in me a seeker, not unlike herself.

My parents named me Mary Lucille after both my grandmothers. Mary, my mother's mother, was sweet and conservative, a traditional mother and wife. Lucille was a maverick entrepreneur who did not conform, who defied all rules made for women and was seen as quite a rebel in our family. My parents chose to name me Mary first, I think, to offset the Lucille in me some way. To make the sour sweet.

At the end of her life, Lucille had achieved success beyond her wildest dreams, but the payoff was anything by sweet. She lost her business, and her husband and her children had drifted far from her, resentful of her always putting business first above them. How quickly a triumphant story of hard work and determination became a cautionary tale. Can a woman truly have it all? Her life served as lesson for me for years; yet now I understand her so much more, including her struggle to balance—achieve yet nurture, succeed yet stay soft and warm.

For better or worse, even back then on the beach, I knew that this would be a struggle within me for the rest of my life. I was Mary who took after her namesake and kissed Papa gently on his forehead before sneaking out the door to be Lucille. Jump ahead to today, and I'm still turning this thought around in my brain. Is that what we do as women, I wonder? Try on different roles and see which one "fits"? And once we pick out our "perfect" role, are we committed to it for life? Heavy questions for someone who slings tiny hot dogs for a living, I know . . . but I also know that as a businesswoman and now a mom, I'm just as proud of my Mary moments as I am of my Lucille moments. I want to believe that instead of struggling with which one to be, I can celebrate them both, Mary and Lucille, like a perfectly mixed cocktail, honoring what it means to be a modern woman, and forever struggling to find that magic formula, that secret blend.

I remember once going into Lucille's bedroom and seeing a huge stack of romance novels by her bed. Night after night, people clamored to be in her presence, but it was love, true love, that Lucille desired most. Upon reflection, this always makes me sad. I was young when she died, but I find myself falling in love with her more deeply as I have grown older. I think I understand Lucille more than anyone in my family. On *Inside the Actors Studio*, host James Lipton gives guests a chance to answer the question, "If heaven exists, what would you like to hear God say when you arrive at the pearly gates?" I somehow feel that when I get springboarded to the next party, as it were, it will be Lucille who greets me at the gate. The ultimate hostess there to let me in. I'd tell her thank you, that she was loved, deeply loved by me. And I get it. Until then, I'll continue to ask everyone who'll pull up a chair to listen, "Do you want to hear a story about an incredible woman named Lucille?"

# That's All I Need

I have this dream of one day leaving New York City and my business and opening a flower shop in a small town near a lake (think *On Golden Pond*). I am soothed by the idea of nothing controlling my workweek but a sign that says OPEN or CLOSED.

On days I felt like being open, I'd turn the sign to OPEN, and when I sold out of peonies or simply wanted to catch a matinee, a quick turn to CLOSED and I would be done. I would post no hours—I'd either be there or not. I would have one employee, an older woman or a gay man, who too loved flowers and storytelling, who also lived a "biggish" life but wanted more simplicity. We would sit in the shop, drink coffee, cut stems, and talk about how lucky we were that we got out of our stressful careers when we did and how we could never go back to those long hours and sleepless nights.

The plan has evolved over the years, from a flower shop to what is currently a flower shop in the front and a ten-seat bar in the back. I would love to be a florist by day, bartender by night, and writer during the in between. Around when I hit forty, this plan hit its stride and became almost a hobby. At night before bed, I find myself doing real estate searches in places like Lake Rosseau, Canada, and now, thanks to Netflix, the Ozarks. I google-map their Main Streets, seeking the location for my shop.

By the way, this is very different from the things I used to search for on the internet. In my twenties and thirties, my searches included fantasy apartments or the cost per night of the hotel in Cabo where Gwyneth Paltrow was staying. But something changed over these last few years. We all think the grass is greener in other people's neighborhoods or if *x* happens, we will be happier. Well, my career has shown me some great, great lawns (and penthouse terraces and the interiors of private planes), and at one point I realized that if I didn't start loving my life for exactly what it is in the moment, then everyone's grass would always appear greener. I started to notice that a lot of people who we assume have it all struggle with the same insecurities and unhappiness that plague everyone. More is not more fulfilling. Bigger is not better. You can order all the caviar in the world and still be hungry. You can be the king of your dinner table but not want to go home to your castle. Please don't misunderstand me. I'm very fortunate that my business supports me; that my family is healthy; that I didn't cut bangs last year. Yes, with age comes wisdom, but also, if you're lucky, humility.

Those who know me roll their eyes when I talk about my flower shop bar in the Ozarks. "You'll never leave New York, Mary. You'll never slow down. You're just too restless. You're always on to the next thing." And maybe they're right, but hey, they also rolled their eyes when I told them I was going to be a caterer, write a book, and be on TV. So let's just see what happens, but please, keep your ears open for Peonies and Palomas on Main Street: flowers in the front, drinks in the back. I may be coming to your town.

## Frozen Palomas

I prefer Blanco tequila here, and if this truly is my bar, then I prefer Casamigos.

MAKES 2 DRINKS

.................................

2 ounces tequila

4 ounces freshly squeezed grapefruit juice

2 ounces fresh lime juice

2 ounces agave syrup

3 cups ice

.....................................................

Mix all ingredients in a blender and serve. Looks great with a drink umbrella, my favorite drink accessory.

## Acknowledgments

Thank you, Running Press, especially Kristen Green Wiewora, for taking a chance on an aspiring storyteller with an affinity for salted meats and melted cheese. You are a truly talented editor, and I hope this is the first of many collaborations we will work on together. PS: I still love you even though you still haven't seen *The Jerk*.

Thank you, Abbe Aronson—editor, publicist, and lipstick aficionado—for always helping me find my words while also crossing my t's and dotting my i's. You are a true dream weaver.

Meg Thompson, the best book agent on the planet. Thank you for believing in me and for being the first person to call me a writer and making me believe it. Can't wait for our next big adventure.

Joanna Adler, for giving me the confidence to share my stories and helping me find them. We will always have Feathers, Jackie Green, and our summer of mold. You are magic.

Michele Pokowicz, my business partner, my rock and the best in the business. Thank you for not only supporting me on these creative journeys but encouraging my dreams, no matter how silly or wild they may be. I stand in awe every single day of the amazing that you are. Cagney and Lacey, Lucy and Ethel got nothing on us! Thank you to Carol Pokowicz for creating a superhuman daughter, and for your delicious meatballs.

Ryan Brown, my business partner and Captain though rough and calm seas. Since the day we met, you have protected me and made me feel safe. You are a true professional, an honest and good man, and I'm so grateful for you every single day!

Michael Fiore and Eric See, for being the culinary magic that is MGCE. Thank you for turning my stories into food and my dreams into reality.

To my MGCE family (Robson Demattos, Samantha Siciliano, Paige Vincent, Tyler Misenheimer, Ilana Schackman, Christopher Sloan, Chris Cadenelli, Allison Norby, Jennifer Weisfisch, all my amazingly talented waiters and chefs, and everyone else who stopped by along the way). How lucky I am that you chose me. I'm so grateful that I am allowed to bask in all your creative energy. One of my greatest joys is being part of your stories as you pitstop with me on the way toward realizing your dreams. I hope they all come true.

To all my loyal clients, especially those who helped give me my start: Cindy Tenner, Molly McCooey, Frank and Michele Rella, Keisha Escoffery, Denise Rich, Bradley Cooper, Peggy and Mickey Drexler, and Jessica and Jerry Seinfeld.

Tara Littman Reilly and the *New York Magazine* gang that allowed me to finally Eat My Stories! Tara, your support since the way-back days is *everything*!

Ayler Young and Keith Weckstein and all the OG's at the Tribeca Film Festival, for giving me my first big break.

My real-life Lady Lobsters: Stefani Masry, Annie Nugent, and Chudney Ross. You ladies lift me, inspire me, make me laugh, make me cry. You are forces of nature who each entered my life as true blessings. My stories mean nothing if I can't share them with you.

Lydia Fenet, twenty years ago, we embarked on a professional journey together that very quickly turned into one of the most empowering female friendships I'll ever know. I'm so proud that I can call *The Most Powerful Woman* in the Room my favorite dream collaborator.

My ladies . . . and Tripp: Cindy Haliburton, Adrien Broom, Pearl Aday, Reyna Mastrosimone, Anne Thornton, Adrienne Schlow, Mallory Page, AJ Birchby, Grace Potter, Allison Tavel, Kelly Powers, Lisa Vogel, Jennifer Rubell, Lauren

Cohen, Lara Gad, Elizabeth Mccarthy, Ashley Burr, and Tripp Swanhaus.

Tara Fogarty-Graziano and Tommy Crudup and the entire gang at *The Rachael Ray Show.*

Jay Alaimo, if I die tragically, please delete every single text exchange we've ever had. That's all.

Rachael Ray, there will never be a thank-you that is bigger than your heart. Thank you for sharing your magical world (and John and Izaboo) with Ryan and me.

Ina Garten, how lucky I was to share a moment with you. Thank you for being a true inspiration and lady who supports ladies!

Lee Blumer, you are with me every day. Alex and Bari, I'm grateful you are in my life.

The Langs (all of you), for teaching me the meaning of "chosen" family.

My beautiful family, who make the stories of my life that much richer: Uncle Frank and Aunt Carol Nicchi, Aunt Therese Jarmain, and my beloved Uncle Richard Jarmain, our family poet.

Brian and Scott Jarmain, my Brothsins (brother-cousins) and your beautiful families. I am who I am because of how much you two loved me and made fun of me.

Christopher and Carrie Ann Nicchi, how lucky we are to have so many wonderful stories. You guys have my heart forever. Don't every stop believing in the magic that is Chester.

Cousin Greg, my hero sandwich. You have sparkled since the first day I held you in my arms.

My goddaughter, Lucy Nugent. You take my breath away with your kindness, beauty, and intelligence. Thank you for loving Gala the way you do.

And my sweetest baby goddaughter, Eloise. I can't wait to watch you grow and be a part of your story.

Dr. Barad, for looking me in the eyes and telling me that I would be a mother someday—and truly meaning it.

To our selfless, loving, and precious family in North Carolina, who gave us, through God's guidance, the greatest blessing I will ever know. Talk about a story!

For all my Endosisters who suffer from Endometriosis and all the women who long to find their little person. I hear you, I feel your pain, you are not alone.

Veronica Bazan and your beautiful family: thank you for loving and caring for my little girl the way you do.

Charles, Pamela, and my beautiful sister Sophie, for your true love always.

Tess Giuliani, a.k.a. Gigi, for adding beautiful color to our lives.

My best friend, my rock, my sister, Nanette. I would need a whole other book to thank you for all you have done for me and given me that makes my life happy, special, and complete, especially my incredible brother Eugene and my dearest loves and godchildren—Luke, Cole, and Mia—who make me laugh, smile, sing, and dance every day!

My parents, Robert and Nancy, who taught me how to eat, pray, and love with GUSTO!

Ryan, my one true love. Our story has no end.

Gala Lee, you will forever be my greatest story. The greatest words I ever heard spoken were on the day you called me your mama.